r

Dogs

Dogs with Charm and Personality

Color photographs by well-known animal photographers

Drawings by Renate Holzner

Consulting editor: Fredric L. Frye, DVM, MSc, FRSM

BARRON'S

Contents

*Preceding page:
Young Tibetan
terriers. When
full-grown, these
dogs look like a
small version of
the bobtail (see
photo, page 12).
They need the
same grooming
as the Lhasa apso
(see page 76).*

*West Highland
white terrier
("Westie") sitting
up on its hind legs
and begging.*

Preface

Small dogs are more popular today than ever before. Who could resist the way they come up to you with their noses upthrust at a jaunty angle and their little tails wagging vigorously? But however diminutive they may be in stature, all of these dogs have strong, well-defined personalities, and they also want to be treated accordingly. All too often, owners of small dogs fail to realize that. They relegate their pet to the status of a lap dog and a "toy," not taking into consideration that the animal's physical and mental health can suffer profoundly from such treatment.

In this Barron's pet owner's manual, Armin Kriechbaumer, an expert on small dogs, explains everything the owner of such a dog needs to know. You will learn the essentials of buying a dog, preparing "customized" meals, keeping your pet in good health, and grooming it daily.

On *How-to* pages you will find information—accompanied by step-by-step drawings—on housebreaking a puppy and training a young dog properly. After all, even the cutest little dog needs firm, consistent training. And to keep your pet physically fit, there are also games and exercises—"tailor-made" for small dogs.

In the *Portraits* section, popular breeds of small dogs are presented in photographs, along with detailed information on their general appearance, size, weight, coat, color, temperament, grooming, care, and breed-related problems.

The authors and the editors of Barron's series of nature books wish you a great deal of pleasure with your small dog.

Please read the "Important Notes" on page 95.

3

What You Need to Know About Small Dog Breeds

Young Pomeranians look like tiny balls of wool.

How the Small Breeds Originated

Nature has always produced a great variety of dogs—large and small, long-haired and short-haired, quiet and lively. We humans have profited from that diversity by selectively breeding dogs with a certain external appearance and certain character traits with each other and "creating" more and more new breeds over the course of time.

Small dog breeds came into being for various reasons. In earlier times, some small dogs, such as dachshunds and Yorkshire terriers, were employed for very specific tasks by hunters. Others, like the Pekingese, Shih Tzu, and Maltese, were created as "live toys" for the salons of well-to-do ladies of the nobility. Every land in the world has produced its own breeds of small dogs, which in time, as a result of the trade among nations, became known in other countries as well. The Chihuahua, for example, comes from Mexico, while the Pekingese and Shih Tzu originated in China and Tibet. Many terrier types were bred in the Scottish Highlands. Even in ancient Greece, dogs with clipped coats and lionlike manes were known to exist. They might be the ancestors of the petit chien lion or of the poodle. Hairless dogs were indigenous to the Aztec kingdom and China. The descendants of these dogs include, for example, the Chinese crested hairless.

In previous times, owning an expensive purebred dog was a privilege reserved exclusively for the aristocracy. That situation changed with the French Revolution in the eighteenth century, when privilege based on social class was called into question. Wealthy members of the middle class began to call attention to their prosperity with expensive pedigreed dogs that could be distinguished at a glance from mutts. The demand for purebreds soared.

Clubs, Associations, and Breed Standards

The English realized quite early that only strict regulation of breeding could ensure the purity of a given breed. Breed or specialty clubs were established. The first dog show in the world was held in England in 1859, and after that breed clubs were founded in a great many other countries as well. They all had the same goal: to standardize the typical features of each and every dog breed. Many breed descriptions were written around the turn of the century.

In the official breed standards, every breed is described from head to toe, and its height, weight, general appearance, and character traits are set down exactly. The standard specifies how the ideal representative of each breed should look. Because nature does not permit complete uniformity, however, a standard can only present a goal to which breeders need to come as close as possible. Unfortunately, the prescripts of many standards also call for things that are unhealthy and unnatural for a dog. For example, we

A close friendship has grown between this rottweiler and the Yorkshire terrier.

breed dogs whose legs are so short that they can no longer walk normally. Noses that have been bred to be excessively short hinder the dog's breathing. There are dogs whose eyelids are curled up, so that their eyes lack protection of any kind.

Responsible dog clubs and associations work against excesses of that kind. They are concerned primarily with preserving the given breed in its substance and characteristic features and excluding breeding defects. That is why stud books record breeding particulars in such detail. By drawing up a pedigree, or genealogical table, that pertains to each purebred dog, breeders can establish who the parents, grandparents, and other relatives of their dog were. The titles their dogs win at shows are also recorded in the pedigrees.

Responsible dog clubs train breeding supervisors, who closely scrutinize anyone who wants to breed a dog. For example, they examine the state of the premises and inspect the type of kenneling provided for the animals.

Tip: Make sure that you buy a dog whose pedigree bears the mark of the American Kennel Club. Reputable associations and breeders adhere to the strict regulations of this organization.

At shows put on by dog clubs and associations, the results of the breeding programs are presented, and dog judges rate the animals in accordance with the prescribed standard. The cream of the crop can aspire to the title of champion, provided their owners show enough perseverance. At the national and international levels, titles can be earned only by attending a multitude of shows.

The Difference Between Large and Small

Basically, small dogs differ from large ones only in terms of size. Apart from that, a small dog is emphatically a regular dog. It does not need to be overly coddled, because it is untrue that small dogs are more susceptible to disease than large breeds. On the contrary, their life expectancy is even higher on the average. Depending on the length of your pet's hair, coat care is just as time-consuming as for a large dog. Small dogs do not need to be constantly carried around in your arms. If correctly trained, they also are capable of amazing accomplishments. Even the short-legged Shih Tzu, for example, can easily manage walks of several miles.

Nonetheless, small dogs have a decisive advantage over large ones. They can be happy even in a cramped city apartment, while for a large dog that would be a cruel fate.

In playful scuffles such as these dachshunds are engaged in, puppies determine their comparative strengths, which can establish their subsequent standing in the pack.

Buying a Dog and Its Basic Equipment

What to Consider Before You Buy

Unfortunately, all too frequently small dogs are bought on the spur of the moment. Their engaging appearance leads many a dog lover into making a rash, imprudent purchase. At home, the initial enthusiasm for the new member of the family quickly

Rules of Thumb for Choosing a Breed

- The smaller your apartment, the smaller the dog should be (see Portraits, page 63).
- Dogs that have very short legs and a long back (such as miniature dachshunds, pugs, and Pekingese) have trouble going up and down stairs. Ground-floor apartments or apartments accessible by elevator are more suitable for them.
- Active dogs need a great deal of space.
- Stubborn, powerfully built, or lively dogs need a human "pack leader" who is firm and consistent. Otherwise, life together can become an ordeal for both parties.
- In dealing with children, some dog breeds are particularly good-natured, while others are extremely touchy. Dogs that tend to be nervous and fearful are the wrong choice if you have children.
- Older people would be wise to pick dog breeds whose nature is reputed to be quiet and easy-going.

flags. For instance, it vanishes once it starts to rain and no one wants to take the dog out to relieve itself. You need to consider thoroughly, therefore, whether you really are able and willing to offer the dog everything necessary to its welfare.

The following questions should help you reach the right decision:

1. A healthy, well-groomed dog has an average life expectancy of 10 to 15 years. Are you prepared to accept the responsibility for it for that length of time?

2. Do you have enough time to take daily walks with your pet and spend time with it? You need to allow one or more hours a day for those activities.

3. Are you sure that your daily routine will stay as it is now? A dog should never be left alone, for example, for more than four hours a day.

4. You may get sick or have to take a trip. Will you have "foster parents" available to take care of your dog at such times?

5. Can you afford a dog? Dog food, veterinary fees, license fees, equipment, and accessories may cost several hundred dollars annually, depending on the breed.

6. Does your landlord approve of your plans to keep a dog?

7. Is any member of your family allergic to dog hair? (See Important Notes, page 95.)

8. Are you willing to change some of your personal habits when a dog joins your household? If you like to sleep late, for example, a dog that has to be taken outside early in the morning to

Your pet should always wear its dog tag and an address holder with the name of the dog and the owner's name, address, and telephone number.

relieve itself will quickly become a nuisance.

9. Do you have enough patience to accustom the animal to its new home?

A Male or a Female?

If you would like to breed your dog, it is best to buy a female, or bitch. Apart from that, your dog's gender is a matter of personal preference. As far as keeping a dog is concerned, the only relevant differences between a bitch and a male are as follows:

• A bitch is in season twice a year, and during this time she is able to conceive. Estrus, the period of sexual receptivity, is accompanied each time by bleeding, which lasts for about 10 days. To keep the female from soiling anything in your home, have her wear a sanitary garment and pad (available in pet stores).

• Males are always in the mood for romance. That becomes obvious whenever you take a walk and there is a female in heat in the vicinity. In addition, the male leaves "scent marks" everywhere; he lifts his leg and releases a few drops of urine to assert his claim: This is my territory!

Tip: It is not true that males are more aggressive and less affectionate than females. That depends entirely on the personality of the individual dog.

When a Second Dog Joins the Household

From the beginning it is obvious that a dog does not necessarily need another member of its species in order to feel happy. Normally, it accepts your family as its "pack." Naturally, however, it does enjoy playing and tussling with another dog.

Most compatible are a male and a bitch. Keeping a pair, however, has one great drawback for the dog owner. When the bitch is in season, there is no way to control the male. To prevent unwanted

offspring, you need to either have the bitch spayed or the male castrated.

Two females often do not get along very well.

Two males first have to work out their hierarchy; that process inevitably entails some fighting. Once their ranking is clear, they usually can live together without difficulties.

The Second Dog: What Breed Will Work?

Can a large dog and a small one live together amicably? Yes, as a rule, because big dogs instinctively show consideration for little ones. Furthermore, small dogs react very adroitly and avoid potential dangers. Among the small dog breeds, I know of some that do not go well together. For example, nasty disputes may arise between a Lhasa apso and a Yorkshire terrier. In general, however, all the small dog breeds get along splendidly with each other—assuming the dogs are in good mental health and have good character traits and behavior. The dog owner's capacity for empathy (resulting from correct training of the dogs) also plays a large part in the ability of two different breeds to live together without friction.

In conclusion, a few universally valid rules:

• Don't get a second dog if the "apple of your eye" has a passion for fighting or tends to bite.

• To keep the dogs from becoming jealous, you need to treat them both exactly the same.

• Choose dog breeds that are similar in temperament. For example, if your dog loves exercise, give it a companion that also likes to be active.

Small Dogs and Other Pets

Cats: The legendary hostility between dog and cat is not inevitable if your home is large enough for the two to be able to keep out of each

When buying a dog, don't let yourself be guided too much by "love at first sight." Take plenty of time to select a puppy. Look the dog over carefully, and test its behavior.

The bichon frisé is intelligent and has a cheerful, open manner.

other's way, if the dog and the cat grow up together, or if you bring a young kitten into a house where an adult dog lives.

Cats and dogs that have lived in the same house for some time do take on a "house smell" that is imperceptible to our senses but is responsible for their accepting each other eventually. A puppy and a kitten will get along fine in most cases, learning enough of each other's "language" in play. Occasionally they may become so attached to each other that they choose to sleep together.

On the other hand, antipathy between the two animals may be so great that peaceful coexistence is simply not possible despite your most patient efforts, and the problem will become far greater if you try to integrate a dog into a "cat household" with more than one cat.

Other pets: While the dog is young, there will be few problems for the time being, but once it enters "puberty," as a rule it will start to hunt guinea pigs, dwarf rabbits, hamsters, squirrels, mice, and birds. Its innate urge to hunt will drive it to kill its supposed "quarry."

HOW-TO:
Legal Matters

What Does the Dog Liability Insurance Policy Cover?

The liability insurance policy always helps out when the risk connected with the animal has become a reality. The dog that suddenly runs across the street and causes an accident is insured, as is the dog that fights with or bites another dog, or pulls a bicycle rider off his or her bicycle and causes injury.

As a rule, however, insurance does not cover a dog that is misused as a weapon and employed wittingly and purposefully against humans. Then it is not the risk connected with the animal that materializes, but the imposed will of a human being.

For additional information on legal matters related to your dog, contact the American Kennel Club (see address on page 95). A call to your lawyer also may be helpful.

What Is the Dog Owner's Liability? Who Is Liable If Children Are Out with the Dog?

Even with a well-trained dog, it is not completely impossible that the animal will enforce its own will and cause damage. Liability insurance for dog owners, therefore, is an absolute must if you want to avoid such claims to damages due from you or members of your family.

In the United States, laws may change from state to state and even from county to county. Dog owners always should obtain detailed information regarding canine laws and canine insurance in the area they live, especially if they moved there recently.

Most people like dogs, and small dogs are less capable of creating a legal problem than large ones. These are two statements in your favor. However, you must prepare for the unexpected.

When and How Long May a Dog Bark Indoors or in the Yard?

If a neighbor feels that dogs are causing such a racket that the normal sound level is exceeded, he or she can demand forbearance from the dog's owner and, if necessary, can even achieve that objective by legal means. This holds true even when it is a watchdog that is being kept. Some courts have decided that the barking of the animals always infringes on the neighbor's legal status as a property owner. Here it is immaterial whether the dog's barking exceeds a certain sound level. Noises that attract attention are always irritating infringements, even if they fail to exceed the sound level at which even traffic and industrial noises are still tolerable.

There are, however, steps that you can take to avoid the problem from the start:
• Determine what causes the dog to bark.
• Be alert to stop the barking as soon as it starts. Dogs learn.
• Train your dog to respond to a command to be quiet. Try saying "Enough!" with emphasis.
• Reward your dog whenever it barks for watchdog reasons.
• Don't leave the animal unattended for long periods of time.

Dogs in Rented Apartments: What Are the Dog Owner's Rights and Duties with Respect to the Neighbors?

Whether a dog is allowed in a rented apartment or not depends first and foremost on the rental contract.

In contrast to small animals (canaries, golden hamsters, etc.), keeping small dogs in an apartment is not absolutely safe as far as the laws governing tenancy are concerned. If keeping an animal is fundamentally prohibited in the rental contract, you can scarcely get around this ban; the prohibition is operative and entitles the lessor to terminate the lease without notice if necessary.

The matter is judged differently if the rental contract specifies that keeping a dog is contingent on the permission of the landlord. The jurisprudence on this complex of problems currently can be summarized as follows: "Dog with good manners allowed." That is, the right of the tenant to the uninterrupted development of his or her personality includes the keeping of a dog. A dog that does not actually bother the other tenants usually does not constitute a use of the rental apartment contrary to the terms of the contract, not even if the rental contract specifies that a dog may be kept only with the lessor's permission. Rather, it has to be proved in each individual case that the keeping of a dog does in fact represent an unreasonable nuisance (noise or unclean conditions, for example) for the other inhabitants of the building. The mere presence of a specific clause in the rental contract stating that keeping an animal is not allowed does not constitute a sufficient prohibition.

In the case of an owner-occupied apartment, a general prohibition against keeping a dog fundamentally cannot be adopted. What is permissible, however, according to at least one judicial authority, is a decision by all the owners to the effect that the keeping of pets in owner-occupied apartments is to be restricted to a reasonable number of animals. Thus, for example, the right to limit an owner to one dog and one cat may be conceded.

In the United States, rural v. urban attitudes toward pets do play an important role. What people in North Dakota may decide and do will significantly differ from New York City dwellers. Therefore, it is always wise to check the details with a lawyer.

Is There a Municipal Law That Dogs May Not Dirty the Street, Or Is This a Community Issue?

Dog excrement should not be left on the sidewalk, yet this call of nature cannot always be avoided. Fines for the person walking the dog can be the result, as judicial authorities have affirmed that an abstract danger to public health exists when sidewalks are dirtied by dogs relieving themselves. This is based on the medically substantiated fact that dogs can carry certain diseases. Moreover, the dirtying of sidewalks by dog excrement also presents a threat insofar as it can result in pedestrians' slipping and possibly injuring themselves. Even worse, if you let your dog deposit its feces on a playground with a grassy area or in a grassy area used for sunbathing and fail to remove it, this constitutes a breach of regulations according to some municipal statutes—failure to remove ecologically hazardous waste.

Tip: To remove the dog excrement, use the handy disposable scoops for dog droppings (available in pet stores), for example.

Motion Studies
These photos show how greatly small dogs enjoy running, jumping, and playing. That is why you should occasionally give in to your dog's urge to be in motion and allow it to let off steam in open country. Before you let it off its leash to run, however, the dog needs to have learned to come when called, and also should obey the command "Sit."

This Yorkshire terrier is not afraid of "big animals." It jumps bravely over the huge dog's back

An open-air outing from time to time does not relieve you of the duty of taking daily walks with your dog, of course. The walks, which are essential to its well-being, provide an interesting change from life in your apartment and give your pet an opportunity to gain new impressions.

This young Maltese is airborne: All four feet are off the ground.

Wind doesn't bother

With its ears flying, this poodle races after a ball.

Make it possible for your dog to spend some time with others of its kind. Growing dogs in particular learn social behavior by playing, romping, and engaging in playful disputes about rank with other dogs (see page 36).

This Maltese's hair fans out around it like a veil.

the Tibetan terrier.

The Italian greyhound has an unusual way of sprinting.

HOW-TO:
Equipment

Before you bring the dog into its new home, you have to do some shopping for it. Your new pet needs the following:
- Sleeping basket or cavelike bed
- Blanket
- Two dishes or bowls (for water and dog food)
- Dog food
- Leash and collar
- Address capsule or name tag (see drawing, page 7)
- Toys
- Pet carrier

practical, because they are machine-washable.

For short-haired breeds, I can also recommend small wicker baskets. Long-haired dogs, however, get their coat tangled in the ends of the wicker, and when the animals try to get free, hairs are very likely to be pulled out.

Blanket: As padding for the bottom of the basket or bed, I recommend an easy-care blanket or heavy bath towel folded to fit the bed. Washable pads that can be disinfected are available by mail order (see Addresses, page 95), and are better than any wool blanket.

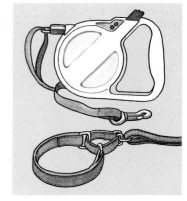

2. Above, a retractable leash with a brake button; below, a collar with a choke ring.

ers attach felt pads to the inside of the collars, and over time the felt will rub off the hair of long-coated dogs.

A collar with a choke ring is depicted in the drawing. It can be very helpful, especially for walking strong or slightly larger-than-average breeds of small dogs. You need to take a close look at the choke mechanism of such collars, however. If you use the collar improperly, you can hurt the dog.

The retractable leash gives the dog quite a large radius of movement. You can keep the leash short or, depending on its length, let several yards unroll. Retractable leashes with a length of about 10 to 16 feet (3–5 m) are completely adequate for small dogs.

1. For sleeping and as a place of refuge, small dogs like cavelike beds. Made of plushlike material, these beds are machine-washable.

- Grooming tools and equipment (see chapter on grooming, page 43)

Cavelike Bed
Drawing 1

Most small dogs feel quite comfortable in a cavelike bed to which they can retreat at any time. Pet stores offer them in a variety of styles. Cavelike beds made of plush or pile are very

Collar and Leash
Drawing 2

The leash and collar have to be selected with the dog's size and strength in mind.

A suitable collar for small dogs is a lightweight leather or textile version. Make sure the fit is not too snug. Of course, the collar also can't be too large, or the dog can slip its head out. Incidentally, many manufactur-

Food and Water Dishes
Drawing 3

The basic accessories should include one bowl for dog food and one for water. The bowls or dishes should be made of stoneware, ceramic, or stainless steel.

14

I highly recommend containers that have "rubber feet" on the bottom to keep them from being pushed around the room when the dog eats or drinks.

Not recommended are plastic dishes for dog food—first, because they slide around too readily; second, because they can be damaged by the dog's teeth. Swallowing bits of plastic can seriously impair your dog's health.

Pet Carrier
Drawing 4

A pet carrier is a practical acquisition. These carriers are extremely handy on trips or for visits to the veterinarian.

Owners of Yorkshire terriers who take their dogs to participate in shows can cover the carrier with a velvet throw and use it as a "display pedestal" on which the Yorkie can stand for presentation to the judge. Pet carriers made of plastic or fiberglass are available. The plastic carriers are cheaper, but they have a drawback in that they are too hot in summer.

3. Food dishes of stainless steel or ceramic are ideal.

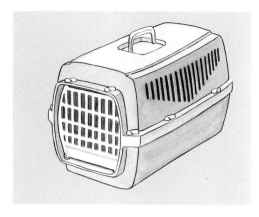

4. On trips or when going to the veterinarian, your dog will be safe in a pet carrier. Models made of fiberglass are recommended.

Fiberglass carriers, which really are a better choice, are unfortunately not yet widely available in pet stores.

Toys
Drawing 5

Not only young dogs, but adult ones as well enjoy whiling away their time with entertaining games. Pet stores offer an enormous variety of toy designs to keep them amused.

All toys made of solid rubber or rawhide are suitable. Dogs also enjoy boisterously pulling a piece of natural-colored rope or an old sock through the house.

Unsuitable are toys made of plastic (see Food and Water Dishes, page 14) and objects that are so small that they can be easily swallowed.

Dog Food
Many breeders give their customers some of the dog's accustomed food to take along when they pick up their new pet. Nevertheless, to be on the safe side, ask the breeder ahead of time what the dog is used to eating, and have a supply of the

dog or puppy food, as well as some dog biscuits on hand in your pantry (see Feeding and Nutrition, page 45).

5. Toys give the dog some diversion.

A noise has attracted the attention of these King Charles spaniels.

A Dog and a Baby—Can It Work?

It can, if the "master" and "mistress" don't give their pet any grounds for jealousy. The dog will treat the baby like a puppy that it has to protect and defend. The widespread belief that dogs are a source of infection for children is untrue. Of course, if you are expecting a baby, you need to have the dog examined by a veterinarian, just to be safe. In addition, pay close attention to good hygiene. Later, the child will acquire a natural immunity to many pathogens.

Nevertheless, it should go without saying that the child and the dog will not eat "from the same plate," lick each other clean, or sleep in the same bed (see Playing, page 34).

Where to Buy Your Dog

Breeders are the best source for a purebred dog. Contact the puppy placement offices of the associations responsible for the individual breeds (for addresses, see page 95). The breeders whose names they supply are subject to the constant supervision of the breed associations and their respective parent organization (see page 95).

Good pet stores will be glad to assist by giving you addresses of reputable breeders. (Breeders who operate in accordance with the breeding guidelines of the American Kennel Club, see page 95.)

Hobby breeders and dog owners who are not members of any organization usually advertise their dogs for sale in daily newspapers or in trade publications, under the classified heading "Pets, Livestock, & Poultry." Always read such ads with a very critical eye.

Don't buy your dog from a mail-order source or from "breeders" or dealers who cannot show you the puppy's mother and who provide only vague information about the dog's background. Often these poor animals come from "puppy mills" or importers. Generally they are disease-prone, and not infrequently they are mentally disturbed and may display behavior that is unacceptable.

The Age of the Puppy When Bought

Responsible breeders place their puppies in new homes when they are nine to 12 weeks old. By then the process of weaning and separation from the mother is complete, and the puppy is increasingly interested in its environment. At this age it usually can get settled in a new home without difficulties, and you can begin training your new housemate, step by step (see page 25).

Tip: If you plan to exhibit your pet at dog shows, you might do better to buy a slightly older dog. The breed characteristics required in a show dog develop only as the animal grows older.

The Puppy Test

The time has come. You have found the right breeder, made yourself comfortable in his or her living room, and you are surely feeling somewhat excited. Now you are shown a puppy that charms you right off the bat. Then you may find a second one or third one appealing as well. You are becoming confused by now, because all the little puppies are equally sweet. This is the moment to take a closer look. Scrutinize the puppy's outward appearance first, then its behavior.
• The coat should not look dirty and unkempt. Dogs whose grooming has been neglected to that extent may be more disease-prone.
• The eyes should be clear and bright, not stuck together.
• Dirty ears are either a sign of sloppy grooming or a symptom of possible illness.
• Are the puppy's teeth all right? This is important if you would like to breed the dog.
• If the dog is a male, both testicles should be descended into the scrotum.
• A distended abdomen is an indication of worm infestation.
• Does the puppy have difficulty moving around? There are many breed-related diseases that become even more pronounced later on. Don't touch such a puppy with a ten-foot pole.

Test 1: How Does the Puppy Behave Initially?
The aggressive type is lively and energetic from the very start; it comes right to you. The cautious type holds back a little at first and doesn't open up until it has taken a closer look at the situation. The scaredy-cat type crouches trembling in a corner, and nothing can persuade it to come any closer to you. Don't buy a puppy that is overly fearful; it may have behavioral problems that can be remedied only with a great deal of patience and understanding.

Test 2: How Does the Puppy React to You?
Try to get the puppy to notice you. Squat down, coax it to come to you in a calm voice, and pat the floor gently. If it comes running up inquisitively, that is a good sign. Such a dog has a straightforward manner and will later become an attentive companion. Next, carefully pick up the puppy. Most little dogs feel comfortable with that right away. Others become restless, because they are unaccustomed to the way you lift and hold them. Have the breeder show you the right way to do it.

When buying a dog, always have a detailed contract of sale drawn up. If legal disputes should arise later, the contract will serve as an important piece of evidence in court.

Test 3: How Does It Act When Playing?

Some dogs play wherever they happen to be at the moment. They always find an opportunity to make the most of their innate play instinct. The presence of strange humans, however, can result in more subdued behavior. Use a little ball to test the puppy's willingness to play. Let the ball roll past the puppy. A dog with healthy development will run after the ball.

The Contract of Sale

However much you are looking forward to taking the new family member home, don't forget to have a detailed contract of sale drawn up. Responsible breeders always have such contracts on hand at home. The contract of sale needs to contain the following information:

Remove ticks with special tick nippers or tweezers. Rotate the tick to remove it (see page 40).

• Name and address of the buyer and the seller.
• Information about the dog (breed, name, whelping date, stud book number, and possibly a tattoo number).
• The dog's state of health upon delivery, including faults, if any.
• Faults that affect the breed standard, such as an atypical hair color, malocclusions, hernias, and the like.
• Purchase price and method of payment.
• Method of delivery (in person).
Along with the contract of sale, you will receive the dog's vaccination certificate (see below) and its pedigree (see page 6).

Important: Vaccination Certificate, License, Insurance, Tattooing

Vaccination certificate: It constitutes proof that your dog has been immunized against the major contagious diseases (see vaccination table, page 55).

License: Almost all communities impose a dog license tax, the amount of which depends on the nature of your residential district (rural area or large city). Consult someone at city hall to find out the age at which your dog has to be licensed. The regulations vary. Along with the official notice of assessment, you will receive a dog tag, which the dog has to wear (required in many towns).

Insurance: Just to be on the safe side, you should take out a dog liability insurance policy or have a rider added to your homeowner's coverage. Small dogs also break away from their leash on occasion and may even cause an accident. The expenses you then would incur could be considerable. For several years now, some insurance companies have also offered health insurance for dogs. Depending on the amount of your premiums, the costs of various treatments given by your veterinarian are reimbursed in part or even in full (see Useful Addresses, page 95).

Tattooing: Some breeders who belong to the American Kennel Club (AKC) prefer to have their dogs tattooed with a coded number (usually on the ear, more rarely on the inside of the thigh). One of the reasons for instituting this procedure was the constantly increasing number of thefts of purebred dogs. Dogs that have run away, however, also can be identified easily by means of the tattooed numerals and returned to their owners. An alternative solution that does not rely upon a visible tattoo is to have a tiny microchip, encoded with your dog's individual identification, implanted by a veterinarian. The microchip is invisible, easily "read" by a hand-held device, and costs very little.

Dealing With Your Puppy

The Right Time to Bring It Home

It is best to choose a Friday for picking up the little puppy at the breeder's home. Then you have the entire weekend ahead of you, and you can get the puppy used to its new home at your leisure, showing your new pet the attention and affection it needs.

For the little dog, this is the beginning of a period of total readjustment. It has had to leave its accustomed pack, which includes the breeder's family as well, and everything it experiences after the moment you pick it up is new for it.

If you plan to bring the puppy home by car, you should have a second person with you. The little dog will withstand the trip with far greater equanimity if it is allowed to lie on your companion's lap and be stroked. Keep a hand towel or a roll of paper towels within reach, because all the excitement the puppy is experiencing can easily wear such a little animal's nerves to a frazzle. It may throw up or "tinkle" during the trip.

Tip: If you can't find anyone to come with you, or if you have to rely on public transportation, it is best to put the dog in a pet carrier (see drawing, page 15) or a carryall—left unzipped, however.

This puppy is clutching its favorite toy, a solid rubber ball, firmly between its front paws. While playing, puppies need a rest break more frequently than adult dogs.

Important: Make sure the dog is not in any drafts; it would catch cold.

The First Few Hours in Its New Home

Depending on its temperament, your dog may start to "reconnoiter" by sniffing the unfamiliar surroundings immediately after reaching its new home. Let it do as it likes. However enticing it may be now to keep picking up the little creature and "cuddling" it, don't give in to temptation. The dog needs time for its reconnaissance missions.

Also, at the beginning, keep the puppy from becoming an "object on view" for your friends and acquaintances. Urge your children to avoid making any unnecessary noise. All this interest would be too frightening for the little animal. Limit yourself to stroking it lovingly and speaking to it gently. That will calm the puppy and make it approachable.

Important: If you are a first-time dog owner, you first need to "dog-proof" your home. For example, conceal electrical cabling. Puppies, in particular,

How about a little tussle?

No objection here.

often bite through electric cables, and the result may be a fatal jolt of electric current. In this connection, please see the list of potential hazards on page 31.

Its name: Undoubtedly you have already chosen a name for the little puppy. Its name needs to be short and concise. Address the puppy by its name from the outset, and use it to call your pet to eat, play, or come to you. It will quickly understand that it is supposed to answer to this name.

Its sleeping place: On the How-to pages "Equipment and Accessories" (see page 14), I described the kind of cavelike bed and little basket that would be suitable as your dog's habitual bed. For its location, select a corner in your home where the dog will not miss anything, but still can be undisturbed. The spot should be free from drafts and cold air at floor level, and the bed should not stand right in front of the central heating or the radiator, because the heated air will make the dog's coat too dry. At night, a room temperature of 64.4°F (18°C) is ideal for sleeping. Show the little newcomer its place, but don't force it to lie down there and rest at once. Often the puppy will find itself an additional favorite spot away from the area where it sleeps. It has a preference for places that promise a great deal of entertainment, and therefore variety. Usually that place is the living room sofa. If you let it have a corner there, the dog will be contented and happy. Put down a blanket there especially for your pet, as it is important for the dog to recognize its own smell again. After a short time it will get used to sleeping in the bed you want it to use.

The First Night

During the daytime, the little puppy

In the eighth to twelfth weeks of life, puppies practice patterns of social behavior with their siblings. As they play, they not only test their strength, but also try out modes of behavior—ranging from threatening gestures to displays of affection.

I give up—one of us has to be the winner.

has received so many new impressions that it has forgotten the pain of being separated from its mother and its brothers and sisters. At night, when everything is quiet and the puppy is lying alone, it is often overcome by homesickness. It whimpers and cries heart-rendingly in its basket.

Although its cries undoubtedly will cut you to the quick, don't make the mistake of bringing the little animal into your bed. It will always want to be there from then on, and it has learned how to get its way. Preferably, put its basket next to your bed the first few nights, so that it can sense your nearness, and pet it soothingly from time to time.

In addition, put something of yours—an old, unwashed sweater, for example—in its basket. It will instinctively feel somewhat less forlorn and usually will settle down.

Incidentally, not all dogs "cry." Many small dogs fall asleep at once after a day filled with new experiences, and you can go to bed with an easy mind.

HOW-TO:
Housebreaking

It is certainly important to you to get your little puppy housebroken as quickly as possible. To accomplish that, you need a large supply of time and patience during the first few weeks.

Basically, you need to make it a habit to take the puppy outdoors every two to three hours at first, especially after every

1. As it searches, the dog sniffs around on the floor—an indication that it has to "go."

meal and every nap. If it actually "does its business" there, praise it. Then it will learn two things at the same time: first, that it will be taken outside at regular intervals; second, that it always will be praised if it urinates and defecates there.

The time required. You can't decide ahead of time how much time it will take to housebreak the puppy. That depends both on how consistent you are with your pet and on its ability to learn. You should allow three to six weeks for the housebreaking process.

How to Tell When the Puppy Has to "Go"
Drawing 1

All dogs behave differently when they have an urgent need to "go." These are the most common patterns of behavior:
• A search mode; that is, the puppy runs around frantically, putting its nose to the floor and sniffing.
• It turns around in a circle, as if trying to bite its tail.
• It sits down repeatedly.
• If it has already been outside with you several times, it may stand at the door, scratch at it, and look at you questioningly or pleadingly.

It is essential to watch closely to see when your puppy is ready.

At night the puppy will draw attention by whimpering if it can't scramble over the side of its little basket. It is reluctant to soil its own bed, and its "cry for help" is an attempt to get you to carry it outdoors.

Newspaper for Emergencies
Drawing 2

The process of housebreaking is far from easy at first for

2. If you live on the upper floors of an apartment building, for the time being you need to put down newspaper for your puppy in the bathroom. The little dog can "do its business" on the paper.

dog owners who live on the upper floors of apartment buildings. Incidentally, that is also true of dog owners living alone who fall ill or who temporarily have trouble walking.

By the time you notice that the puppy has to go out, it generally is useless to grab it and quickly take it downstairs to go outside. The puppy won't hold out that long. It will urinate in the elevator or on the stairs, and it won't understand what all the fuss is about. In this case, it is preferable to spread out some newspaper for your pet in a corner of the bathroom or on the balcony, set the dog down on it at the first hint, and praise it once it has been a good dog and done its business. Particularly with male dogs, make sure the newspaper covers not only the floor, but a portion of the wall as well. As you know, an adult male lifts his leg to urinate and is certain to hit the wall when he does so.

It is best to replace the newspaper each time, as soon as the dog has finished using it.

Naturally, the newspaper is not intended to become a

long-term solution to the toilet problem. In addition, go outside with your pet, taking the customary newspaper along at first and placing the dog on it.

Tip: You may think that a cat box filled with appropriate litter is more hygienic than newspaper. Unfortunately, most dogs will refuse to use the box.

A Permanent "Potty Area" Is Important

Drawing 3

Carry the puppy out in your yard or to the street without delay when you see the first indications that it has to go. It is best to take it to the same place every time, because as time passes it will recognize the place again by its own scent. Incidentally, it is not easy to find a permanent place for your pet out on the street. In addition, the street and the sidewalk have to be kept clean, so that leaves only the gutter (see How-to: "Legal Matters," page 10). Make sure the place you select is not one where a great many other animals leave their droppings. Your puppy could become infected by pathogens contained in the feces of other dogs.

If an Accident Happens

Without fail, your little dog will have mishaps from time to time and stain your carpet with tiny puddles and droppings. It does no good to punish the puppy unless you catch it in the very act. Later on, it will not make any connection between the punishment and the forbidden deed. But if you have caught your pet in time, immediately carry it outside or to the desig-

nated spot in your apartment and scold it with a forceful "Phooey!"

Tip: The deplorable custom of hitting the puppy or pushing its nose into its little pile or urine puddle to punish it is completely absurd. Such punishment will even slow the learning process. Only words

3. *Always bring the puppy back to the same place when it is time for it to defecate and urinate.*

of praise after it has done what you ask will promote learning and understanding.

How Can I Get the Rug Clean Again?

Urine that has seeped into the rug leaves an unpleasant odor. It is best to clean the carpet with a weak solution of vinegar and water or with plain soap. The smell will go up the dog's nose and be unpleasant, which will keep your pet from using the same spot again.

Tip: Never have a urine-stained rug dry cleaned; wash it instead. After application of dry-cleaning chemicals, an unpleas-

ant smell associated with the urine will linger in the carpet.

If the Dog Forgets Its Training

As a rule, a dog will remain housebroken once it has been trained to avoid excreting indoors. Sometimes, however, it may suddenly resume doing its business at "off-limits" places in your home. What brings about such lapses? There may be several causes. First have your veterinarian rule out any disease-related cause. The second possibility is that your pet has an emotional problem. Then you have to investigate to determine what has disturbed your dog's emotional balance. Some possible causes are changes within your family, jealousy of a baby, or a move that the dog has been unable to cope with.

Lovingly, this mother dog takes care of her little puppy.

Adapting to Different Food

Even if you have brought along some of the puppy's usual dog food for the first few days, it may refuse to eat and may even develop diarrhea. More uncommonly, the puppy even throws up. That may be due to the exciting events of the past hours. I recommend that you use a tried-and-true household remedy in such a situation:

In my experience, puppies will readily eat a boiled potato, salted lightly and mixed with some seared ground beef (without fat).

Sometimes, bland foods like rice gruel or thin oatmeal will also help.

Don't force your dog to eat, however. Usually, the stomach upset will improve in a short time. Watch for other symptoms in your dog. If you are in doubt, have the veterinarian take a look at your pet.

If the little dog contentedly goes back to its playing, however, and if its eyes are bright, there is no reason for any great concern.

Dog Training—
Made Easy

The domesticated dog views its "human family" as its pack. What otherwise would be the job of its parents now falls to you to perform, such as training the puppy to be a companionable, self-assured dog that finds life a joy. Basically, if too many people participate in the training at the same time, it will confuse the dog, and behavior problems may result. Within a family, whichever person can show the greatest consistency and patience is the one best suited to train the dog. All the family members, however, should agree to use the same training commands.

Tip: On How-to pages 26 and 27, you will find a list of the major objectives of the training process.

Basic Rules of Training

• Train your dog while you play with it. It learns more readily in that situation.
• Change the inflection of your voice when you praise or reprimand your dog.
• Discipline that comes too long after the misdeed will have the wrong effect. The dog always draws a connection between the discipline and whatever it is doing at the moment.
• Never punish the dog by striking it. A sharp rebuke or the act of smacking your hand or the table with a newspaper will seldom fail to have the desired effect.
• If the dog has done a good job, shower it with tender words of praise and stroke it. Little tidbits (dog biscuits, for example) reinforce a lesson that has been successfully learned.

Bad Habits—How to Break Them

If you vacillate when training your dog, you will later have to battle all kinds of bad habits that the dog has acquired. The attempt to break an adult dog of bad habits does not always culminate in success.

Begging at the Table
Every dog owner surely is familiar with this situation. The food is on the table, the dog looks at you with pleading eyes—and your heart melts. If you give in now to its plea for a morsel from the table, it is all over. Your pet will never again give you any peace until you share some of your food with it. That means you need to remain "tough." You will be doing both your dog and yourself a favor. The fact is that spicy foods will do lasting damage to its health (see Feeding and Nutrition, page 45). Get the dog used to staying in its habitual spot while you and your family have your meals.

Another helpful hint: Divide your pet's daily ration of dog food into two servings and, if possible, give it one when you yourself are about to eat. Then its begging will be curtailed because it is occupied with the dog food in its own dish. If it is an extremely determined beggar, hold a piece of onion or lemon under its nose. These "scents" are revolting to dogs, and your pet probably will take to its heels as quickly as possible.

A cotón de Tulear puppy. Reputedly, dogs of this breed are always in a good mood and are a constant source of entertainment for their family.

HOW-TO:
Training

If life with your dog is to be free of problems, your pet needs to learn several things and to obey certain commands. Except for housebreaking (see How-to, page 22), it is futile to begin these exercises before the puppy is three months old. Dogs are easiest to teach between their fourth and sixth months of life, although adult dogs too are still capable of learning.

Walking on a Leash
Drawing 1

For walks together with you, it is crucial that the dog learn to walk on a leash (lead).

To train your pet to the leash, first, show the dog its collar and leash and let it sniff them thoroughly. During the next few days, keep putting the leash on your pet for short periods, and

1. Practice "walking on the leash" by carefully pulling the dog along with you and pointing in the direction you want it to take.

watch the dog as you do so. At first it will try with all its might to take off the unaccustomed object. Later it will forget about the collar, because it will have gotten used to it.

Walking "on the leash" is something you need to practice with your pet inside your home. This kind of "false imprisonment" will certainly not please the dog at first. It will offer resistance by fighting against the leash, turning around in a circle, or lying down stubbornly on the floor. Some dogs also react fearfully or yowl. That will improve with time. At first, move in whatever direction the dog wants to take. Bit by bit, urge it into the direction you choose. Once the dog has taken a few steps in the right direction, shower it with praise.

The first walk in the park or in street traffic will not be devoid of problems. A young dog is easily diverted by the unusual sounds and smells. If that happens, carefully pull your pet along with you, and at the same time point your hand in the direction you want it to go. If it obeys, don't forget to praise and pet it.

Quite soon after the first walk, the dog will stop battling the collar and leash. It now knows from experience how much diversion and adventure a walk signifies for it.

Tip: While you are training the dog to the leash, a short leash is better than the retractable one (see How-to, page 14).

The Command "Sit"
Drawing 2

When you stop moving and utter the command "Sit," the

dog should sit down. It is not allowed to leave its place until it hears the release command "Go." This exercise is important when crossing streets, for example, or when you want the dog to wait for you in front of a store. Practice this command during walks. Pull slightly upward on the leash and gently guide the dog's hindquarters down into a sitting position. Once your pet begins to understand what is being asked of it, praise it extensively. Repeating

2. Practice the "Sit" exercise by pulling up on the leash slightly and gently pushing down on your pet's hindquarters.

the command two or three times during the course of a walk is sufficient.

The Command "Let Go"
Drawing 3

The purpose of this command is to get the dog to give you whatever it has in its mouth, such as your new shoe, which it is in the process of dragging blissfully through the apartment. On walks, too, it can

3. The command "Let go" directs the dog to give you something or stop doing something.

be very helpful if the dog obeys this command. Quite frequently, as you know, dogs pick up things that can be harmful to their health. If you want to take something out of your pet's mouth, gently hold its nose still and press its lips lightly against its teeth. As you do so, give the command "Let go." If it drops the object, pet and praise it as a reward.

Coming When Called

Your dog should come happily when you call. Before you can let it off its leash to run in open country, however, it has to follow this command "in its sleep," so to speak. At first, practice in your apartment and in the yard. At the start, always reward the dog with a little tidbit if it heeds your call. Then it always will associate something positive with your summons, and it will come racing up gladly. Later on, a few pats will be sufficient reward for its good behavior.

Following to Heel (off the Leash)

Only when the dog can walk on the leash without problems, has mastered the command "Sit," and comes when called, is it all right to practice letting it off the leash. The objective of this exercise is to teach the dog to walk along at your side as if it were wearing the leash, following your every move. To practice, look for an area that you can survey easily, not close to a busy street or woods.

First, take the leash off the dog as unobtrusively as possible, and give it the command "Heel!" If it leaves its place, call it back immediately. If it continues to walk at your side like a good dog, praise it lavishly. The dog will not understand at once what you expect of it. Here only continuous training will help.

The Command "Stay!"
Drawing 4

A dog that is not wearing its leash should remain lying or come to a halt immediately upon hearing the command "Stay!" uttered while you stand some distance away. Obeying

this command can be very useful in certain dangerous situations, for example, in order to stop the dog at once. It often happens that the dog wants to run across the street in an unguarded moment, perhaps to greet another dog, or because something else has aroused its interest. The dog will certainly not learn the command "Stay" overnight, however. It is one of the most difficult exercises. It is advisable to practice this command together with other exercises in an area used for dog sports or in a dog training school, under the direction of an instructor.

4. The command "Stay" tells a dog that is off its leash to halt or remain lying wherever it is at that moment.

The Dog Chews on Everything

Young dogs in particular like to chew on firm objects to make the process of cutting teeth easier. Unfortunately, they stop at nothing—not even furniture, rugs, and shoes. If you catch your pet "red-handed," put a stop to its activity with a firm "No!" Pet stores carry special sprays to use on the things that have been chewed. Bitter apple is an example of such a product.

The smell of these sprays is designed to prevent the dog from any further chewing. It is best to give your pet a bone made of rawhide, on which it can chew as long as it likes. Don't make the mistake of giving the dog an old shoe in place of the new pair on which it may have been chewing. How is a dog supposed to decide which shoe is new and which is old? It will keep right on chewing on all shoes.

This miniature griffon puppy is looking somewhat sulkily at the world around it.

Jumping Up on People

Whenever I visit my sister, her little silky terrier greets me effusively. It jumps up on me and tries to give me a wet "kiss." On the one hand, I am glad that it wants to give me such an exuberant welcome, but if it has just been outdoors and I end up with paw prints all over my new white pants, I am annoyed. The dog's behavior, however, is easily explained. It is innate; this is the way a puppy greets its mother, to wheedle her into feeding it.

Many dog owners do not object if their dog always greets them with such enthusiasm. They simply interpret it as a great proof of their pet's love.

Visitors, however, usually think such behavior is bad conduct. Here again, make it your policy to nip things in the bud. As soon as a young dog tries to jump up on you, hold your palm outstretched toward it and ward it off with an uncompromising "Stop it!" or "No!"

There are various ways, however, to keep from dampening its enthusiasm over your arrival:

• Whenever it tries to jump up on you, stop it with a firm "Sit!" If it obeys the command, praise it and pet it as much as you like.
• You also can divert the dog from its effort to jump up by keeping a small ball ready and rolling it on the ground, for example. The dog is sure to chase after the ball. When the game is over, reward your pet with a little tidbit (see Appropriate Feeding and Nutrition, page 45).

Common Behavior—Rubbing Against Your Leg

Most dog owners find it embarrassing when their dog wants to act out its sexual drive by rubbing against their legs or the legs of friends and their children. That is understandable, because this bad habit is annoying. Here again, it is up to you to be consistent and firm from the very beginning. As soon as your dog tries such behavior, ward it off with an uncompromising "Stop it!" or "No!"

Children and dogs often become inseparable friends. Dogs also are of definite learning value for children. By dealing with them, children acquire a sense of responsibility and duty and learn thoughtfulness and consideration.

A child can be a playmate and "someone to bond with" at the same time.

Daily Life With Your Dog

Humans and dogs don't speak the same language, of course, but they are able to understand each other. Over time, you will learn to interpret the varied body language and articulate language of your pet. The dog bases its understanding of what is expected of it on its owner's tone of voice or gestures.

Unfortunately, humans and dogs do not speak the same language. Nevertheless, it is amazing to see how well dog owners and their pets get used to each other's ways over the course of time. Dogs understand what their master and mistress want of them by guessing their thoughts from their behavior and tone of voice. And owners understand their dogs as well—after all, they learned early on to correctly interpret their pet's pleading look or the friendly wag of its tail.

Typical Behavioral Patterns

A dog can make itself understood to "its" human in two ways: by articulate language or by body language.

The dog's articulate language encompasses a wide repertoire. Barking, snarling, whining, whimpering, and growling are sounds that we can readily classify. You will quickly find out whether your dog is barking because it is happy or because something is upsetting it. Whimpering can mean that the animal feels ill or believes it is being treated unfairly. It is more difficult to understand the various intermediate sounds correctly. That requires a great deal of empathy and close observation on the part of the dog's owner.

Body language is another means of communication employed by dogs. You can figure out a great deal by looking at your pet's ears, particularly if it belongs to a breed that carries its ears erect. If the dog is excited or if something is arousing its special inter-

est, its ears will stand bolt upright, or even vibrate with extreme concentration. Even when the dog is asleep, it has its "antennae raised" to pick up every movement and every sound. "No unusual occurrences," the dog reports, by slightly relaxing the upright position of its ears. Ears that are laid back—and in many breeds, folded over as well—mean increased caution and a "wait and see" attitude, sometimes also a desire to attack.

Dog breeds with drooping ears, too, can employ similar modes of expression. Although a hanging ear is heavier as a rule, the ear muscles, depending on the dog's mood and its degree of watchfulness, cause the ears to rise and fall at the point where they are attached.

The movement of the tail is coordinated with the play of the ears. Watch your dog someday while you play. You are about to throw a small ball to your pet. The tiny animal stands in front of you with its muscles tensed, its little legs planted firmly on the ground, and its ears and tail pointing straight up.

A tail carried parallel to the ground is a sign of contentment. If it is carried at a slight angle and also wags slowly from side to side, completely tensed, the dog is indicating that it is not altogether sure of its ground, but if necessary it will not seek to avoid outright conflict. Excited wagging of the tail, however, means that the dog is tremendously happy. A tail tucked under is a signal of anxiety and uncertainty, and if the dog lowers

Hazards in Your Home and Yard

Source of danger	Possible effects	How to avoid
Balcony	Dog may fall.	Install safeguards (Nets are available in pet stores.)
Chemical weed-killers, pesticides	Poisoning.	If the dog uses the yard, don't use any chemicals of this kind. Slug/snail poison, in particular, smells tempting to dogs, but has a fatal effect.
Electrical cables	Dog may bite through the cord and. receive an electric shock	Conceal cords; don't leave exposed cables live; unplug everything when you leave the house. Keep a close eye on puppies, in particular.
Plants	Poisoning, injury.	Don't keep poisonous plants in your home or yard. Examples: laburnum, lilies of the valley, naked ladies, ligustrum, rhododendron, foxglove; gold dust plant. Immediately vacuum up any fir needles dropped from your Christmas tree.
Broken pieces of objects, nails, sewing needles	Cuts on the toes and pads of the feet; dog may also swallow foreign objects.	Clean up carefully; don't leave dangerous objects lying around.
Jumping down from relatively high seats.	Broken leg; in the worst case, a broken neck	Never leave the dog alone on the sofa or chair when you leave the room. Yorkies like to jump, but cannot estimate the danger of a given height.
Electrical outlets	Electric shock.	Use childproof covers, available in electrical supply stores.
Steep or open stairs	Fall, concussion, or skull fracture.	Carry the dog; don't let it climb stairs alone. Watch it closely.
Doors	Being squeezed when door is opened; being locked in or out.	Keep an eye on doors; keep them closed if there is a draft.
Detergents and cleaning agents, chemicals	Poisoning, acid burn if licked.	Store all chemicals safely in cupboards.

Danger of falling: If a small dog falls off the balcony, it can be fatally injured. Installing some kind of safeguard on your balcony is a must!

its head in addition, that indicates a guilty conscience.

Tip: The expressiveness of the dog's body language may be lessened, depending on the length and shape of the tail (curved, long, short, curled, docked).

Marking and Sniffing

As stated in the chapter Buying a Dog and Its Basic Equipment (see page 8), male dogs mark their territory by urinating on tree trunks, posts, or poles. If a predecessor has already left his "visiting card" there, your dog will sniff at it and then cover the odor with his own scent mark. On walks, let your pet sniff and mark extensively; that will reinforce his self-confidence. Females are interested in the males' scents only just before and during estrus (see page 59). They lay no territorial claims of their own, and for that reason generally leave behind no scent messages.

Digging and Scraping

You will frequently have a chance to watch your dog burying bones or relatively small objects in the ground. This innate behavior had some practical significance for the dog's ancestor, the wolf. Wolves buried whatever remained of their prey's flesh after they feasted, in order to have something in reserve and to let it ripen. Domesticated dogs have no need to lay food in store in order to survive as they are fed regularly. Consequently, many dogs forget where they have buried something, although others note the place exactly and dig up the bone at some later time, with great pleasure.

A dog scrapes at length in its little basket before it lies down to sleep. In this way it builds itself a cozy nest for the night. This behavior, too, originated with its ancestors, the wolves, which in the wild had to scrape out a hollow in which to sleep.

With its unmistakable mane, the bichon frisé resembles a tiny lion.

The Daily Walks

Walks are compulsory exercise for every dog owner. They give your pet the opportunity it needs for physical activity. It can relieve itself at its leisure, has some diversion, and gets new impressions. The dog, however, is not the sole beneficiary of the walk: You, too, will see how quickly your own well-being is improved by fresh air and exercise.

The length of the walks depends on the dog's age, constitution, and breed. There are lively small dogs, such as Yorkies, poodles, and pinschers, that adore running and show incredible endurance. Even short-legged dogs like the Shih Tzu can manage 6-mile (10-km) walks at one go. Others, including the pug, Pekingese, and miniature dachshund, prefer a more leisurely pace and short walks. Lively breeds with a good constitution need to be walked about two to three hours a day, while quieter breeds are satisfied with one and one-half to two hours.

Walking in the Woods

A walk in the woods, with its multitude of different smells and noises, is as exciting to a dog as a good mystery novel is to you and me. You will be surprised to see how much of the hunting instinct there is in your small dog. It will want to track every scent that it picks up. For that reason, it is better to leave the dog on its leash in the woods. The retractable leash (see page 14) allows it enough freedom of movement. For other reasons, too, I urge you to use the leash. You will always be able to keep your pet in your field of vision, and, if need be, you can intervene. Dogs like to pick up all kinds of things that are not always beneficial to their health, such as poisonous plants (see list of hazards on page 31). Moreover, it is necessary to show consideration for other walkers, bike riders, and joggers.

This young schipperke is tugging friskily at its leash. A little outing may be in the offing.

Walking on a Leash

The inexperienced puppy perceives a collar and a leash as shackles that restrain its freedom. To prevent this negative reaction, you should let your dog get used to these objects by playing with them indoors. Put on the collar and walk the puppy around, holding it loosely by the leash (but only after it has had a chance to sniff these things at its leisure). Do this playfully and periodically, and the puppy will end up accepting them in the spirit of play. Once this stage has been reached, you can practice outdoors. Before long, the dog will associate the leash with happy times.

Tip: As a precaution, have your dog wear a tick collar. After every walk you have to search its coat and feet for ticks, burrs, thorns, and sharp little stones (see drawing illustrating tick removal, page 18; see also page 40).

HOW-TO:
Playing

These days our pet dogs scarcely have an opportunity to get enough physical exercise, much less to cultivate their urge to hunt. They need some kind of substitute activity—playing games.

1. "Fetching a stick" is enormous fun for many dogs.

They will chase enthusiastically after a small ball or retrieve the little stick that you throw. Playing keeps the dog mentally and physically fit, promotes a good relationship between you and your pet, helps along the process of training the animal (it learns as it plays), and gets rid of built-up aggressions.

Games That Dogs Like

Does this situation sound familiar to you? Your dog has its front feet flattened to the ground, its chest is touching the ground, its hind legs are bent, and its hindquarters are thrust up in the air. At the same time it is moving toward you in jerks, looking at you very encouragingly, as if to say: "Come on, start playing with me at last." And that is just what it wants. Here are some suggestions for games that dogs especially enjoy.

Running in a circle: You run in front, while the dog runs after you. Move in a circle, changing direction frequently. The dog has enormous fun doing the same thing as its master or mistress. Never ask too much of your pet when playing, however. After a short time, both of you need to take a break together.

Letting yourself be caught: You run away, and the dog runs after you. Keep switching direction as you run. While you play, you also will be training your pet to respond.

Wrestling over a "quarry": The "quarry" might be an old rag, for example. Hold the rag in front of your pet's muzzle. The dog will take it in its mouth. Now pull carefully on the other end of the rag. Don't tug too hard, however, because young dogs' little teeth are still somewhat loose, and they could fall out. After a certain time, you can let the dog move away with its quarry. When it brings the rag back, praise it. Then a new round of play can begin.

Friendly scuffling: Lie down in the grass. The dog will jump all around you, possibly placing its paws on your chest. Gently ward it off with your hand, then ruffle its coat on its chest and nape.

Playing hide-and-seek: Hide behind a hedge, for example, and call your dog. It will pick up your scent at once and greet you enthusiastically when it finds you. Shower it with praise, and pet it lavishly. If you make the game too hard for the dog, however, it will lose interest and be disappointed.

Tracking: Show the dog a tidbit (a dog biscuit or a small piece of meat), then hide the tidbit behind a tree or a bush, for example. The dog has to wait until the food has been hidden. The command "Seek" calls it to pick up the scent. When it finds the treat, praise it. Don't make the game too complicated, or the dog will be frustrated.

Throwing sticks and balls: Most dogs are crazy about this game. The sticks and balls have to be large enough that the dog cannot swallow them. Also make sure that the ends of the sticks are not too sharp; otherwise, the dog can injure itself seriously.

Tip: Never lose your authority as "leader of the pack." If you

2. In dog sports, the animals have to negotiate obstacles. Here, a small dog is jumping through a rubber tire.

do, your dog will assume that position in future. If the dog is getting too big for its boots, put an abrupt end to the game with a stern "Quit!"

Fetching a Stick
Drawing 1

Throw a stick of wood, and at the same time give the dog the command "Fetch!" Arrange it so that the dog has to jump over a low obstacle, such as a tree trunk, when it retrieves the wood. If it brings the stick back to you, praise it and pet it.

Dog Sports
Drawings 2 and 3

Most small dog breeds are capable of amazing athletic feats, and they also enjoy demonstrating their prowess to you. For them, sport equates to play. That becomes especially clear when the little animals are trained at a special dog-training ground or in a dog school under the direction of a leader. This sport for dogs and their owners, which is quite new in this country, comes from England and America. It is known as "Agility." The local groups of the respective breed clubs will be happy to tell you where to find such training areas or schools near where you live.

At the training location, owners and their dogs negotiate a course that is "larded" with obstacles of widely varying degrees of difficulty. For example, the dog has to jump a series of hurdles, jump through a tire, "balance" across a plank, crawl through a fabric tunnel, and walk across a seesaw.

Tip: Some small dog breeds, including miniature poodles, Chihuahuas, Yorkshire terriers, and cavalier King Charles spaniels, especially enjoy practicing little stunts—but don't force your dog to do so. Your pet's behavior will tell you whether it enjoys learning stunts. For example, if it repeats

3. This obstacle is constructed in the form of stair steps, and the dog has to "balance" over a kind of plank.

of its own accord certain sequences of movements that you have taught it, you can safely conclude that it enjoys this type of game. The dog also knows, of course, that it can expect a reward, such as a treat or some petting, when it shows off its ability.

When Children and Dogs Play Together

The pedagogical value of a dog to a child's development is undisputed. The child learns to show consideration for other living creatures and develops conscientiousness and thoughtfulness.

Dogs, however, can be very gruff and touchy in their reactions to children if they don't feel in the mood to play just then. Caution is in order:
• if the dog is in a resting phase at the moment,
• if it is eating, or
• if the dog is still young.

Also make sure that the child does not pull the dog's tail or ears, pinch its coat, or stick a finger in its eyes.

Dog's attitude and ear position are signs of extreme alertness.

This ear position reveals an easing of tension.

Encountering Strange Dogs

If your little pet is to develop in a healthy manner, it is crucial that the dog have contact with others of its kind. That is the only way the little animal will have an opportunity to learn proper social behavior. When two dogs meet, their encounter follows well-established rules:

• Nose contact is, so to speak, their way of greeting each other. By sniffing at each other's nose, they determine whether they will take a liking to each other.

• The second ritual is the anal check. The dogs sniff each other's hindquarters (see drawing, page 50), where the anal glands are located. These glands provide each dog with information about the other. A male lifts his leg immediately afterward, to let the other dog take in his special scent mark and commit it to memory. During the anal check in particular, it very quickly becomes apparent whether the dogs like or dislike each other, or feel indifferent.

If they like each other, the dogs wag their tails vigorously. If they are indifferent, neither takes any further notice of the other. Hostility is accompanied by angry growling, and the dogs may resort to violence.

• Quarrels about rank take place if one dog lays claim to higher standing. To rule out any doubts, a fight ensues, usually accompanied by continual, furious growling, which is, however, intended solely to intimidate the opponent.

Hierarchical disputes look more dangerous to us humans than they really are. The fact is, after only a brief skirmish the weaker dog will acknowledge the stronger by throwing itself down on its back and presenting its throat to its opponent. The stronger dog, satisfied by this gesture of submissiveness, immediately stops fighting the weaker one.

Tip: Smaller dogs very often overestimate their own strength. They consider themselves superior, and for that reason frequently get into dangerous situations. Large dogs that have strong characters recognize that fact very quickly, however, and generally steer clear of snappish little dogs.

Note: The patterns of behavior described here apply exclusively to healthy dogs.

Overbred dogs with behavior problems are unpredictable. They will even bite puppies, although nature has furnished adult dogs with a disinclination to bite where smaller and younger dogs are concerned.

If your pet encounters another dog and you think, for example, that the large dog is seriously maltreating the small one, pick up your dog as a precaution.

Out and About Downtown

If you are planning to take a stroll downtown, you need to consider whether to take your little dog along or whether it might, after all, be better to leave it at home. Keep in mind that in busy streets, your dog—a "half-pint" surrounded by nothing but "giants"— may actually become sick with fear. In addition, down at its level it is forced to breathe the concentrated exhaust gases of the automobiles. If you are willing to carry the dog from time to time, however, there are no further obstacles to your shopping stroll.

The most wonderful aromas will tempt the dog wherever food is sold— and there your pet has to stay outside. Never tie its leash to something out in front of the store, however. Many a time dog owners have returned to find only their pet's leash and collar on the side-walk, with the dog gone for good. For that reason, when grocery shopping, it is better to leave the dog at home.

On public transportation, such as buses, streetcars, and subways, a good solution is to carry the little dog in a shopping bag (always leave it open, so that the dog will get enough air) or in a pet carrier (see drawing, page 15). Ask in advance whether you will need to buy a ticket for your pet. In some cities you will have to pay at least half fare.

Car Trips

Most dogs think riding in a car is great fun. Small dogs prefer to sit on their usual blanket, either on the floor in front of the front passenger seat or on the back seat. Pet carriers (see page 14) are quite safe, even if you

The papillon has learned that this behavior will earn it a dog biscuit.

have to brake suddenly. If you are set-ting out on a long trip, keep the follow-ing in mind:
• If your dog suffers from travel sick-ness or is extremely nervous, get medication from your veterinarian ahead of time.
• When your departure is two hours away, don't let your dog have anything else to eat, or it may vomit during the trip.
• Stop and take a break every one and one-half to two hours. Give the dog fresh water and let it relieve itself.

Contact with others of its kind is crucial to a dog's healthy development. If you have only one dog, you should give it an opportunity to meet other dogs and play with them.

• Always park the car in the shade to keep it from getting too hot inside.
• If the dog has to wait in the car, make sure it has a supply of fresh air. Either leave the car window slightly open or insert a burglar-proof grid (see drawing, page 62).
• If it's all right for your pet to go with you, put its leash on it before you open the car door. Particularly after long rides, the dog wants to get outside as fast as possible, and it will cast all precaution to the winds.

Vacationing with Your Dog

There is no reason not to take your dog along on vacation, but having a perfect vacation depends entirely on how wisely you plan.

If you're going to a foreign country, a vaccination certificate (see page 18) is necessary. Almost all countries require proof of vaccination against rabies upon entry, and sometimes an official health certificate as well. Find out in advance what regulations govern entry into a given country, by asking at the consulate of the country in question or consulting your veterinarian. Some countries, such as England, Sweden, and Norway, require a four-month quarantine. Vacationing there with your dog is not feasible in any case.

If you're going by train, ship, or airplane, you need to inquire at a travel agency or at the appropriate company about the conditions governing transport.

Addresses of hotels, pensions, and camping places where dogs are welcome can be found in travel folders, in brochures sold in pet stores and book stores, or in the newsletters of pedigreed dog clubs.

The "dog's luggage" consists of its usual dishes for food and water; blanket and/or basket; leash; collar; address capsule and dog tag (see drawing, page 7); food supplies, including canned dog food and dog flakes; and a small portable medicine case with remedies for diarrhea and travel sickness, as well as flea powder or spray (consult your veterinarian).

Tip: In some countries, the tap water frequently is not free from germs. Preferably, supply your dog with mineral water (noncarbonated).

If the Dog Has to Stay Home

If you can't take your dog along on vacation, arranging for it to stay with your relatives or friends is best. Your pet will already know the people looking after it and will quickly feel at home.

Members of a dog club can surely find an obliging dog fancier at one of the club meetings who is willing to take care of your pet. At boarding kennels, you need to reserve a place ahead of time, and you should always visit there beforehand to see how the kennel is run. It also pays to ask the breeder of your dog. If enough room is available, he or she will surely be happy to look after your pet in your absence.

How to Properly Groom Small Dogs

You can tell a well-groomed, healthy dog right away by its general appearance. Its coat is glossy, its eyes are clear, and it is well-nourished without being either too fat or too thin (see Feeding and Nutrition, page 45). Its well-being depends on getting expert care that is appropriate to its breed.

Tip: On How-to pages 42 and 43, you will find additional directions for various grooming procedures that you, as the dog's owner, will have to perform at regular intervals.

Coat Care

With short-haired dog breeds, keeping the coat clean and neat is not time-consuming. A few strokes of the brush every day suffice to remove the dead hair. With long-haired breeds, things are far more complicated. The hair becomes matted quickly unless it is carefully brushed out and combed every day, and the coats of many long-haired small dog breeds require professional trimming from time to time (see page 40).

The Daily Combing and Brushing Routine

Such care is important not only because it keeps the coat clean, but also because it simultaneously serves as a massage that stimulates the dog's circulation. Before you start the combing and brushing process, first examine the coat for foreign objects. After a walk, burrs, thistles, pods, and even sharp little stones or splinters of glass can be stuck in the dog's coat.

To learn how to remove ticks and pests, please see the relevant paragraph on page 40.

Short-haired dogs: Using a fine-toothed comb, comb the dog's coat thoroughly (the right way). Next, brush it with equal thoroughness with a brush that has natural bristles. Finally, wipe off minute dust particles and tiny hairs with a damp chamois.

Learning to tie up the hair of the crown takes a bit of practice. First, on each side make a part running from the eye to the ear. Then fasten the strands with a rubber band and a barrette.

Always rinse off the dog shampoo thoroughly.

The "canine coiffure": Long hair on the head—in Maltese and Yorkies, for example—has to be tied up to keep it from falling in the dog's eyes. Tie it together in a so-called topknot (see drawing, page 39). To do so, make a part on each side, running from the corner of the eye to the ear, and gather the hair together above the two parts. Fasten the hair in a ponytail with the help of a rubber band or a plastic barrette (available in pet stores).

The breed standards prescribe a certain style of hairdo for many small dog breeds, including poodles, the petit chien lion, and most types of terriers. If you want to adhere to the standard, the dog has to be trimmed accordingly by a professional dog groomer. Poodles have to go to the dog salon about every four to six weeks, Scottish terriers every six months, and miniature schnauzers in spring and fall.

If you enjoy cutting hair and have a knack for it, you also can learn to perform this demanding task yourself. Get advice at your dog club. There you can also obtain brochures on the grooming appropriate for your dog's breed and guidelines for styling cuts according to the breed standard.

Removing Ectoparasites

Even the best-groomed dog may bring ectoparasites home from a walk (see page 33).

Ticks appear from June to mid-September. Even the slightest contact with a bush or tall grass is enough to brush a tick onto a human or an animal, and it will work its way into their skin with its proboscis, or sucker. Ticks can cause serious illnesses in both you and your pet. You can tell that your dog is infested with ticks by the dark gray to yellowish gray leathery blisters, about the size of cherry pits, that are visible on its skin.

Wire- and long-haired dogs: First, loosen knotted places with your fingers. Then start to give the hair of the crown a good combing with a special brush (first the wrong way, then the right way). When the coat has become supple and smooth, comb it with a special comb (the right way). For some small dog breeds, combing and brushing is not enough: They have to be "stripped" from time to time (for example, spaniels and West Highland white terriers). With your thumb and index finger, pluck the dead hairs out of the coat to keep it from looking dull. In addition, if dead hair is left in place, it can cause excruciating itching in dogs.

Tip: Ask your pet's breeder or your breed club how to take care of the dog's coat and what grooming tools and equipment are needed.

Blow dry the coats of long-haired dogs after bathing.   *Finally, brush the coat of hair carefully.*

After every walk, inspect your dog's coat for ticks. If a tick has gotten a firm hold, grasp it with tweezers or special tick nippers from a pet store and rotate the tool to dislodge the tick (see drawing, page 18).

Fleas can be acquired anywhere by your dog. If it scratches itself with noticeable frequency, particularly its neck and ears, that may point to a flea infestation. When you check its coat, the fleas will be visible to the naked eye. If you don't try to control the fleas, they can cause eczema in the dog. Because fleas, which serve as an intermediate host, can give your dog tapeworm, the dog usually has to be wormed as well. Pet stores sell commercial preparations for external control, including effective shampoos, sprays, and powders (follow the manufacturer's directions!). The dog's bed and all its favorite spots also have to be disinfected, because new fleas will hatch from the eggs the fleas have already laid.

Mites, which appear from August on, affect principally long-haired dogs, causing intense itching (scabies). You will see the mites as tiny light-brown to orange bumps on your pet's skin. Treat the affected areas with a special spray or an antiparasitic shampoo.

HOW-TO:
Grooming

On these How-to pages you will find grooming procedures that all dog owners need to perform on their pets on a more or less regular basis.

Checking the Ears
Drawing 1

For dogs with hanging ears and breeds with a heavy growth of hair, checking the ears weekly is essential. For dogs that carry their ears erect, cleaning the outer portion of the auditory canal every two weeks is sufficient.

Get your dog a liquid ear-cleanser from the pharmacy. With the dropper, place a few drops of the solution in each ear. Once the earwax and dirt have dissolved, carefully clean the ears with a tissue twisted into a point.

Removal of the hair in the ear is a controversial subject. Experience indicates, however, that hairs inside the ear soon are stuck together with earwax and dirt, and bacteria may become established there, resulting in serious ear infections. For that reason, the next time you visit the veterinarian, ask him or her to show you how to pluck the hair expertly.

Tip: Frequent scratching at the ears and shaking of the head may be symptoms of an ear infection or of a foreign body in the ear. Ears that are severely reddened inside or are secreting blackish brown, purulent, or even bloody matter must be treated by a veterinarian.

Tip: Don't forget to regularly comb and brush hanging ears that are covered with hair, as it becomes matted very easily.

1. *Clean the ears with a tissue twisted to form a point.*

Dental Care
Drawing 2

Proper nutrition (see page 45) is a basic prerequisite for healthy teeth.

To prevent tartar buildup, clean your dog's teeth once a week. Either use a toothbrush and specially formulated pet dentifrice (available at your veterinarian's office or in pet stores), or put some calcium carbonate on a cotton pad and rub the dog's teeth with it. If a hard deposit of tartar has already built up, it has to be removed by a veterinarian with the help of special instruments.

Keep a close eye on growing dogs between the ages of five and seven months, when they get their second set of teeth. Frequently the milk teeth do not fall out at the right time. The permanent teeth then grow in crooked behind the milk teeth. If the milk teeth are still too firmly lodged, they have to be extracted by a veterinarian.

Eye Care
Drawing 3

Check your pet's eyes frequently and regularly. Small dogs get a larger share of dust on walks than do bigger breeds. The dust lodges in the corners of their eyes and can cause eye infections if it is not removed. While dogs sleep, eye secretions frequently collect, and they also have to be removed.

Some small dog breeds—the King Charles spaniel, for example (see page 68)—have large, protruding eyes that tear easily. Watering eyes have to be wiped regularly. Otherwise, the tears will leave unsightly stains on the hair just under the eyes. In dogs with white coats, such as Maltese or poodles, these discolorations can be removed only with special preparations (available in pet stores).

2. *Polishing the teeth with a canine dentifrice prevents tartar.*

For eye care, use a lint-free tissue twisted into a point or a piece of absorbent gauze. Soak the tissue or the gauze in fennel tea or distilled water, then carefully wipe the dog's eyes from the inner edge to the outer edge.

Tip: Eye infections always require treatment by a veterinarian.

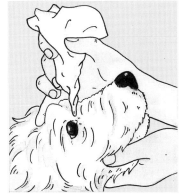

3. Using a tissue twisted into a point, remove dust and eye secretions.

Foot Care

Check the dog's feet every time it has been outdoors. Chewing gum that gets stuck in the hair between the toes is no disaster, but sharp little rocks or tiny splinters of glass can cause the dog excruciating pain.

Keep the hair between your pet's toes from getting too long. If necessary, cut the hair! If the official breed standard is important to you, you will have to take notice of the way the hair is supposed to be cut.

Clipping the Nails
Drawing 4

On floors with soft wall-to-wall carpeting or smooth covering, and even on the sidewalk or the street, dogs' nails cannot be worn down in a natural way. The result: the nails grow too long and, in extreme cases, become ingrown in the balls of the toes, which is quite painful for the dog. Consequently, overly long nails have to be trimmed regularly. For that purpose, use special pet nail clippers (available in pet stores). When you cut them, it is best to hold the paw in front of a light source, to keep from injuring the blood vessels that extend partway into the nails.

Tip: Have your veterinarian clip the dog's nails periodically, or ask him or her to show you how. Breed clubs also demonstrate proper methods of nail clipping.

This part of the grooming ritual is probably the hardest part for most people. Dogs don't particularly like to have their feet fussed with, so learning the correct way from the beginning will save time and keep you and your pet happier.

Occasionally, you might cut a toenail too short and it will start to bleed. Do not get upset. Always keep handy a styptic pencil or a

5. These are essential for coat care: narrow-toothed and wide-toothed dog combs, a wire brush, a currying brush, a brush with natural bristles, an electric hair-dryer, and special shears.

4. When trimming your pet's nails, make sure you don't injure the blood vessels.

quick stick such as men use for shaving cuts and ust it to stop the bleeding. Putting pressure on the foot to walk may start the bleeding again. Have your dog lie down for a few minutes and everything will soon be back to normal again.

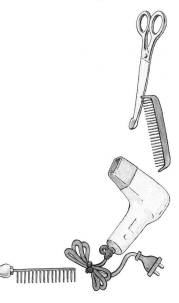

Care of the Hindquarters

At regular intervals, wipe your pet's hindquarters with a damp cloth. Areas soiled by feces not only are unhygienic, but also can cause infections around the anus.

If the dog keeps scooting around the floor on its hind end—a behavior also known as "sledding"—its anal sacs may be impacted and blocked. The veterinarian will have to express the sacs to remove the fluid.

Bathing

Today there are special moisturizing shampoos and rinses for dogs that are formulated for their skin and hair type. For this reason, you can bathe your dog without worry, but only when absolutely necessary (see photos, pages 40 and 41).

The long-haired breeds in particular get their coats dirty quickly when they are walked, when they jump into puddles, and when they dig and scrape in the yard.

Short-haired small dogs need bathing less frequently. Often, thorough combing and brushing is sufficient. A bath is due only when your pet's coat starts to have an unpleasant smell. Especially with short-haired dogs like the short-haired dachshund, a rinsing in clear, lukewarm water is sometimes enough. The fact is that the dachshund's hair contains a fat that has a protective function. Frequent bathing with shampoo makes its hair soft, and that renders it more susceptible to catching cold. Rub your pet completely dry after its bath to keep it from catching a cold. Short-haired dogs can let their coat dry in a warm, draft-free room. Long-haired dogs have to be blow-dried with an electric hair dryer. Be careful not to direct the hot air into your pet's eyes.

Tip: In the portrait section, beginning on page 63, you will find tips on bathing or showering specific dog breeds. See the instructions on grooming.

Daily care of your pet's coat ranks first among the major grooming procedures. Dogs with a long coat of hair have to be combed and brushed extensively to prevent matted hair. Once areas of the coat have become matted, often the only way to get rid of the knots of hair is to cut them out.

Tips on Winter Care

For winter walks with your small dog, you need to take a few precautionary measures:

• Using special blunt-nose shears (see drawing, page 43), carefully cut the hair between the pads of the feet.

• Before the walk, rub the foot pads with vaseline or petroleum jelly to protect them from thawing salt; salt causes pain in the sensitive pads. After the walk, clean the paws with lukewarm water, dry them, and massage them lightly with skin cream.

• After returning home, remove any clumps of snow—particularly if your small dog is long-haired—and blow-dry its coat to keep your pet from catching cold.

• Neither healthy long-haired small dogs nor short-haired ones need little sweaters or coats to protect them from the winter cold, but such garments are quite practical in rain and snow. If your pet wears one, there is no need for the time-consuming blow-drying session. In addition, the snow cannot form little clumps of ice in the dog's hair.

Tip: For long-haired dogs, use only coats made of smooth fabric, such as nylon. Loden cloth or wool cause the hair to become slightly matted.

Appropriate Feeding and Nutrition

A balanced diet of appropriate and varied foods is the essence of good health maintenance. The amount of food consumed also has to be moderate, of course, because dogs that are too fat fall ill and die prematurely.

What Is Appropriate Feeding?

Like its ancestor the wolf, the dog is a carnivore, a meat eater. That does not mean, however, that you should serve your pet meat exclusively. It also needs roughage, carbohydrates, minerals like calcium and vitamins, which are totally lacking or are present in insufficient quantities in a meal consisting solely of meat. The wolf finds a simple solution to the problem. It preys predominantly on herbivores, or plant eaters. It devours them to the last morsel, and in that way obtains the undigested plant matter still present in its prey's intestines and stomach. As a responsible dog owner, you need to make sure that your pet's food contains the right nutrients.

These two Boston terriers appear to be extremely hungry or thirsty.

HOW-TO:
Meals for Dogs

Those dog owners whose hobby is cooking can prepare a banquet for their pet. All they need to know is what nutritional components are essential in a healthful meal for a dog and how the ingredients have to be used, so that the dog gets food of high nutritive value and does not develop deficiency symptoms over time.

What the Meal Must Include

The major nutritional components are:
- protein,
- carbohydrates,
- fats, and
- minerals.

None of the nutritional components listed above should be omitted from a meal you prepare for your dog. The only leeway you have is to vary the flavors, for example, by substituting fish for meat or replacing potatoes with rice.

Protein is found chiefly in meat, fish, farmer cheese, or low-fat cottage cheese.

Carbohydrates are contained primarily in grains, rice, potatoes, kibbled dog food, corn, and also in wheat-based products like bread, noodles, or baked goods. Whole-grain products in particular supply the body with additional vitamins and minerals.

Fats are to some extent found in meat, particularly in pork. If the meat is extra lean, it is best to enrich the food by adding cold-pressed corn, safflower, or canola oil, or vegetable margarine.

Minerals, trace elements, and vitamins have great importance, particularly for young, old, and sick dogs. If you give them commercial kibbled dog food in addition, there is no need to also add a dose of these "vital substances," since they are already present in the kibble. Vitamin and mineral supplements are available in pet stores and from veterinarians.

The Ingredients in Detail and How to Use Them

Meat: Lean muscle meats, such as beef, veal, and horse meat, are suitable, as well as poultry and boned fish filets. From time to time the dog can also have organ meats, including tripe, liver, kidney, and heart. Many dogs are especially fond of these organs, but they

1. Foods to gnaw—including dog biscuits or air-dried pieces of rawhide—are important in keeping a dog's teeth and gums healthy.

should not eat them too often, because they frequently are heavily loaded with harmful substances. (Serve them once a week at most; liver can cause diarrhea.)

It is essential that meat always be served cooked, because raw meat is hard to digest. Never give your pet uncooked pork, because of the danger of toxoplasmosis and other diseases.

• Raw poultry can transmit salmonella. Even the tiniest bone fragments have to be removed from the poultry, because a small dog can choke on them.

The pieces of meat have to be small enough to fit in the dog's mouth. A little piece of meat intended for a Chihuahua or a Yorkie has to be correspondingly smaller than for a miniature schnauzer or a cavalier King Charles spaniel, for example.

Grain (cereal) products: Most highly recommended are whole-grain products. These are suitable if cooked: rice, corn, oat flakes, wheat flakes, and noodles. These need no cooking: stale whole-grain bread, kibble, or even baby food in flake form.

Potatoes: They are always served cooked (unsalted).

Dairy products: Farmer cheese and low-fat cottage cheese can be served just as they come from the store.

Tip: For my dogs, I sometimes stir some grated cheese, such as Swiss cheese, into their food. They are extremely fond of the taste.

Fats: Normally, enough fat is contained in meats. Only if the meat is extremely lean should you enrich the dog's dinner with diet margarine or wheat-germ oil.

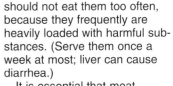

Vitamins and minerals: Either enrich the dog's meal with a commercial preparation of vitamins and minerals (follow the manufacturer's directions!), or add the following to your pet's food: about 0.18 ounce (5 g) of dried brewer's yeast, an equal amount of bone meal, half a hard-boiled egg (finely chopped), half an apple, and half a carrot (raw and chopped in the blender), one lettuce leaf, chopped, and some parsley.

Tip: If you add dog kibble, you can omit the dose of vitamins and minerals. The flakes themselves contain plenty of vitamins, minerals, and trace elements.

Preparation

Let the cooked ingredients cool thoroughly, then mix them with the other components of the dog's dinner.

2. Fat dogs usually are more prone to illness than those of normal weight.

If you notice that your pet is just picking out the chunks of meat, puree the entire meal briefly in a blender. It may be, however, that the dog then will reject it altogether.

Tip: I mix the ingredients with a little meat broth and season the meal with a touch of onion or garlic salt. That makes the dinner irresistible to my dogs. Small additions of salt will not harm your pet's health at all, but the dog may not tolerate other seasonings. Patient and careful experimentation with your pet's taste buds will not only make your dog happier, but it also will foster a closer relationship with you.

The "Dessert"

After the dog has had about two hours to digest its meal, you can give it some "dessert": a few dog biscuits or some veal gristle.

Basic Plan for Home-Prepared Meals for Your Dog

(Stated quantities and ingredients represent one day's rations)

Size of dog	Meat	Fats	Grains	Dairy products
Medium-sized and small dogs (over 10 inches [25 cm] high at the withers)	5.3–7 ounces (150–200 g)	1/2 tablespoon of oil or diet margarine	2.5–3.5 ounces (70–100 g)	1 to 1 1/2 tablespoons
Very small dogs (under 10 inches [25 cm] high at the withers)	2.8–3.5 ounces (80–100 g)	1 teaspoon of oil or diet margarine	1–1.8 ounces (30–50 g)	1 to 1 1/2 teaspoons

Important: Enrich each day's rations with a vitamin and mineral supplement!

Commercial Dog Food

Commercial dog food has definite advantages: It is easy and quick to prepare, and it contains everything required in a healthful diet. It is available in the form of moist, semimoist, and dry dog foods.

Moist or canned dog food (75 percent water) is a nutritionally complete food; it contains all the nutrients that dogs require. Two types of canned dog foods are commercially available:

• Dog food that consists primarily of meat (muscle meat, tripe, heart, liver, and lung).

• Dog food that is enriched with carbohydrates in the form of cereals (rice, barley, oats, wheat, or corn).

The composition is printed on the label for you to read.

Moist dog food should always be mixed with cereal or vegetable flakes to prevent the dog from getting diarrhea (mixing ratio: ⅔ moist dog food, ⅓ flakes).

Tip: Dogs that are given mostly canned dog food must have something hard to bite—dog biscuits, rawhide, or "bones," for example—to keep their teeth and gums healthy (see Foods to Chew, page 50).

Semimoist and dry dog foods, in contrast to canned dog foods, are far more concentrated and higher in energy. Semimoist dog food contains only 25 to 30 percent water, while dry dog food (kibble) has only a 10 percent water content. Your dog needs to have fresh water available at all times, so that it can take in enough liquid.

Tip: Before you serve your pet dry dog food, soften it in unsalted meat broth, unsalted vegetable broth, or water; it will taste better to the dog.

Note: If you would like to "cook" for your dog yourself on occasion, you will find useful tips on How-to pages 46 and 47.

A Chihuahua puppy. The tiny dog stands quite self-confidently on its short little legs.

Guidelines for Buying Dog Food

For a small dog, there is no need to buy large economy-size sacks of semimoist or dry dog food. A standard-size package (usually 4.4 pounds [2 kg]) will do. Once a package has been opened, use it up as quickly as possible, because the vitamins and minerals contained in the food lose their potency rapidly. Opened cans of dog food, too, should not be kept longer than two days in the refrigerator.

Where and When to Feed

Always put your pet's food and water dishes in the same spot. The water dish, however, has to be accessible to the dog at all times, so that it can drink whenever it wants.

Fixed feeding times are also important. It is best to feed an adult dog (12 months and older) its main meal in the morning or at midday (see Bad Habits, page 25), and a small additional portion in the evening. Puppies and young dogs need to be fed between two and four times a day (see Feeding Young Dogs Properly, below).

The Right Amount of Food

Here it is difficult to give universally valid suggestions, because the amount of food depends on the dog's size and weight, as well as on how active it is and whether it is young or old.

According to one old rule of thumb, an adult dog needs about 1.4 to 2.1 ounces (40–60 g) of nutritionally complete food per day for each 2.2 pounds (1 kg) of body weight. Here are a few examples for small dog breeds:

Maltese and miniature pinscher: 7 to 10.6 ounces (200–300 g) of nutritionally complete food per day; pug and Pekingese: 7 to 13.4 ounces (200–300 g); cavalier King Charles spaniel, cairn terrier, and miniature poodle: 14.1 to 21.2 ounces (400–600 g).

"Just where are you?" this cotón de Tulear seems to be asking.

Drinking Water Is Important

Your dog needs fresh water in its water bowl at all times, so that it always is able to quench its thirst. Make sure, however, that the water is not too cold, which could cause it to have diarrhea.

Milk is not suitable for dogs as it also causes diarrhea. If your pet is suffering from a cold, unsweetened herbal tea is a real miracle worker.

Tip: It is hard to say how much a dog needs to drink each day. That depends on a variety of factors, including the nature of the food, the outside temperature, and the amount of activity the dog has engaged in. If, however, a dog for no apparent reason deviates from its usual drinking habits for any length of time, it may be a symptom of illness. To be on the safe side, consult your veterinarian.

Between-meal Snacks

Dog biscuits are meant to be used as rewards and to satisfy the urge to snack, so to speak. Offer these treats sparingly, however, to keep your pet from becoming too fat.

Foods to chew, like dog biscuits, cowhide, veal gristle, or rawhide bones for gnawing, are perfectly all right to give to your dog occasionally. It is even important that your pet have something to chew on, to strengthen its masticatory muscles and clean its teeth.

Tip: Most dog fanciers think they are doing their pet a favor by giving it as large a bone as possible to gnaw on. I am opposed to bones for small dogs, because the tiniest of them all can actually break off their dainty little teeth on them. Moreover, in many dogs bones cause constipation, with results ranging from rock-hard feces to intestinal obstruction (bowel blockage).

Feeding Young Dogs Properly

Food for young dogs has to contain more protein and minerals than that for adult dogs. Pet stores sell specially formulated puppy rations, which I highly recommend.

When you pick up your dog from the breeder, the puppy generally is between eight and nine weeks old. By that time its mother has already weaned it, and the breeder has been raising it on an appropriate diet. Have the breeder give you a few days' supply of the puppy's customary food.

A meeting between dogs proceeds according to well-defined rituals (see page 36).

After that, the process of switching to the commercial product described above is usually not difficult. You also can add farmer cheese, vegetables, boiled rice, cooked whole-grain cereal, or finely sliced fruit to the commercial puppy food. A young dog needs to be fed several times a day:
• four times a day until the age of three months,
• three times a day until the age of six months,
• twice a day until the age of 12 months.

Feeding Old Dogs Properly

We call dogs "old" once they are past the age of 10. An old dogs needs high-carbohydrate foods, which are easily digestible. Old age is precisely the time when the liver, kidneys, and intestines no longer function as well as they once did. Consequently, reduce the proportion of meat in your pet's food and increase the share of rice, pasta, or vegetables.

If Your Dog Is Overweight

Overweight dogs are more subject to illness, and they die earlier than dogs whose weight is in the normal range. Here's how to tell whether your pet is overly plump: Right behind its withers, feel its ribs at about mid-chest level. If the ribs are covered with a thin layer of fat and are easily palpable, its weight is normal. If you can't feel the ribs, your dog is too fat, and you have to put it on a reducing diet. First, eliminate all snacks and gradually cut back a little on the amount of food. Your veterinarian will also provide help and advice, and he or she certainly can recommend a dependable diet food for your dog.

Incidentally, I suggest that you make it a rule to let the veterinarian decide whether your dog needs to go on a diet. Here is a reliable diet recipe, in which the total amount of food per day is approximately equivalent to that given

Important Rules for Feeding

- Always feed your dog at the same time of day.
- It is essential that the food be at room temperature, that is, neither too hot nor too cold.
- Remove any uneaten food from the dish after no longer than 30 minutes. Food spoils quickly, and in summer it draws flies.
- Clean the food dish with hot water after every meal to prevent growth of dangerous bacterial and fungal pathogens.
- Never disturb your pet while it is eating, or it might snap at you.
- From the outset, get your dog used to eating whatever you set before it. Don't immediately serve the dog something else if the meal you first offered obviously doesn't taste good to it; otherwise, it will very quickly turn into a picky eater.
- Some dogs pick only the meat chunks out of their dinner and neglect the rest. Over the long run, that will lead to nutritional deficiency symptoms. If your dog is picky, try this little trick: Puree the dinner briefly in a blender.
- Make sure that fresh water is always available to the dog, so that it can quench its thirst at any time.

in the basic plan for home-prepared meals for your dog (see page 51):
- 50 percent cooked vegetables of all kinds (except potatoes) as a carbohydrate substitute,
- 25 percent cereal bran, alfalfa meal, or dried beet pulp (available in stores that carry organic foods),
- 25 percent tripe as a meat substitute,
- ½ teaspoon of vegetable oil.

Important: Never give your dog meat with fat on it, and use only low-fat versions of dairy products.

Tip: Diet food is also available in commercial, ready-to-use form from your veterinarian or in pet stores.

What the Dog Cannot Eat
- Foods that contain seasonings, such as sausage or table scraps.
- Sweets will damage the dog's teeth and make it fat.
- In most dogs, milk leads to diarrhea. However, buttermilk and yogurt usually are tolerated.

Preventive Health Care and Diseases

The best preventive health care for your dog includes—along with appropriate feeding and good grooming—essential immunizations and regular visits to the veterinarian. Only a veterinarian can diagnose possible symptoms of disease with certainty and help the dog recover quickly.

People repeatedly claim that the small dog breeds in particular are over-bred and therefore disease-prone. Such a blanket indictment, however, is impossible to confirm. Certainly, there are some "black sheep" among breeders, people who, once a breed becomes fashionable, make their dogs into assembly-line machines in order to earn money in a hurry. Puppies that come from such "mills" frequently are indeed disease-prone and have behavior problems. But that applies to all dog breeds, not only to the small ones.

For that reason, let me repeat: If you are planning to buy a dog, choose a responsible breeder. That will save you a great deal of trouble and misery later (see Buying a Dog and Its Basic Equipment, page 7).

Prevention Is the Best Medicine

The basic prerequisites for keeping your dog in good health are, of course, a healthful diet, sufficient exercise, good grooming, and preventive measures such as the essential vaccinations and regular worming. In addition, schedule one or two annual visits to the veterinarian, even if your dog is not ill.

Immunizations

The best means of protection against such devastating infectious diseases as distemper, rabies, hepatitis, leptospirosis, and parvovirus are the appropriate immunizations.

As early as the seventh or eighth week of life, puppies need to be given their basic immunization. To get full immunity, the injections have to be repeated on a regular basis (see vaccination table, page 55). The inoculations are recorded on a vaccination certificate, which you will receive when you purchase your dog. From the vaccination certificate, you also can tell when the dog needs its periodic booster immunizations.

Important: Whenever the dog is inoculated, it should be in good health, and it should have been wormed beforehand. The vaccination schedule on page 55 will tell you when your dog should receive which shots. However, your veterinarian may possibly administer them according to a somewhat different timetable.

Worming

Roundworms and tapeworms can be detrimental to your dog's health; therefore, your pet has to be wormed regularly.

Puppies are first wormed at the age of approximately four weeks, then at six and eight weeks. Ask the breeder about these treatments. Then worm the dog again at 12 weeks, six months, and nine months. Thereafter, worm it only two or three times a year. You can get tablets or pastes for that purpose directly from your veterinarian.

Recognizing Symptoms of Illness

Despite all your preventive measures, your dog may become ill. By this time you are sure to know your pet so well that you will quickly notice if something is wrong with it. Listed below are unambiguous symptoms of illness, clear indications that you should take your dog to a veterinarian as quickly as possible:

• The dog lies around apathetically or creeps into a corner to hide.
• It eats little or nothing, but at the same time it drinks far more water than usual.
• It has a fever and pants virtually without stopping (see Taking Your Pet's Temperature, page 54).

• Its eyes are dull and its nose may be dry. Be aware, however, that some healthy dogs do have warm, dry nose pads.
• It whimpers for no apparent reason or cries out when you touch it.
• It scratches itself constantly, bites at its coat, or shakes its head from side to side.

If these symptoms also are present, see the veterinarian immediately:
• The dog vomits frequently and has fever.
• It has diarrhea, with blood or excessive mucus visible in the stool.

This cavalier King Charles spaniel is walking across the frozen shoreline portion of a lake.

Medicine in liquid form is administered with the help of a disposable syringe (without a needle) or a teaspoon.

Administering medicine: Powders and pulverized tablets can be mixed with the dog's food. Pills can be concealed in a small meatball made with ground meat. If your pet sees through that trick, only the direct approach will help. Open the dog's mouth by gently pressing its chops against its teeth. Place the tablet on its tongue, as far back as possible. Hold its mouth closed and wait until it swallows.

Medicine in liquid form is administered with the help of a teaspoon or a disposable syringe (without a needle). Carefully pull one side of the dog's lower lip downward to create a small "pocket." Just as you complete this procedure, which is unpleasant for the dog, give it a little smack on its hindquarters. Its attention thus distracted, it will swallow the medicine. Powder, dissolved in some water, can be given in the same way.

- Its gums have turned paler than usual.
- If you gently pull up the skin on its body, it "stays there."

How Dog Owners Can Help

It can be very helpful if you master a few important procedures, in case your dog falls ill.

Taking your dog's temperature: If its muzzle is cold (not hot!) to the touch, and if you think its temperature may be higher than usual when you touch its abdomen and the inside of its thigh, you need to take its temperature. Use a nonbreakable thermometer with a digital display. Lubricate its tip with vaseline or cooking oil. The dog should be standing when you take its temperature. It is best for a second person to hold the dog still while you lift its tail and insert the thermometer about .8 inch (2 cm) deep into its anus. Remove the thermometer after about one minute. If the reading is higher or lower than the little dog's normal temperature—about 100.5° to 102°F (38–39°C)—your pet is ill.

Are Canine Diseases Communicable to Humans?

Of the infectious diseases, rabies and forms of leptospirosis are communicable to humans. If your dog has had its shots, there is little danger.

Parasites like roundworms and tapeworms can be transferred from dogs to humans. That alone is sufficient reason to worm your dog on a regular basis.

Fleas and ticks, which attack all warm-blooded creatures, can pass from a dog to a human, but only if they have failed to get a firm hold on the dog's skin.

Fungal diseases are becoming more widespread. They can attack both humans and dogs and are mutually communicable.

First Aid Procedures

Because prompt help sometimes is essential, I offer here a few tips for situations in which your dog's health might be endangered. In addition, see page 95 for a list of books that are particularly useful in emergency situations.

The dog has injured itself: Minor injuries—due, for instance, to the dog's having a splinter of glass or a thorn in its paw—are something you can often take care of yourself. Carefully remove the foreign body from the wound, then clean it. Disinfect the wound with a standard over-the-counter remedy such as hydrogen peroxide (3%) from the pharmacy.

Injuries of a more serious nature usually entail heavy bleeding. In this case you need to apply a pressure bandage. First, without aiming for completeness, remove foreign bodies from the wound if any are present. Next, fold a piece of gauze bandage or clean fabric several times to make a thick pad, then press it against the wound. Bind a gauze bandage around it all fairly securely, but make sure that you do not completely tie off the extremity in question. If the bandage has been tied too tightly, the tissue around it will swell. Check the bandage by slipping one finger under it. If you can do so easily, the bandage is not too tight. Then take the dog to the veterinarian at once.

Bites: It may happen that your dog is bitten during a fight. Sometimes a fairly large blood vessel is severed, and the blood gushes out. Immediately apply a pressure bandage as described above. In an emergency, putting pressure on the vessel with your hand will also be sufficient to keep the dog from bleeding to death. Take it to the nearest veterinarian at once.

Poisoning: Admittedly, it rarely happens that a dog eats poison, but it is possible nonetheless. Even today, some people persist in putting out bait to control rats, for example. Particularly if your dog suddenly begins to vomit repeatedly and has diarrhea, poisoning may be the cause. If so, blood usually will also be visible in the vomit and in the stool. Take the dog to the veterinarian as quickly as possible.

Vaccination Schedule for Preventive Health Care

| | | Basic Immunization | | Booster shots |
| | | Follow-up shots | | |
Acts against	Weeks 7 to 8	Weeks 10 to 12	After about week 12	12 months after basic immunization
Canine parvovirus (live vaccine)	x	x		x annually
Distemper	x	x		x annually
Hepatitis	x	x		x annually
Leptospirosis	x	x		x annually
Rabies			x	x annually

Important: Vaccinations are not effective immediately. It takes one to two weeks for active immunity to develop.

Heatstroke: Short-nosed small dogs in particular, such as the Pekingese and pug, have a tendency to circulatory failure in excessive heat. Older or debilitated dogs also can be thus affected. Cars that are left parked in the sun or pet carriers without an adequate air supply can turn into heat traps. Similarly, too much exercise on overly hot days can lead to circulatory failure. The dog first goes into convulsions, then loses consciousness, and can die if not helped quickly. To give it first aid, immediately lay the dog in the shade or take it to a cool room. If possible, rub it thoroughly with dripping-wet cold cloths. Then take it to the veterinarian at once.

Insect bites: In summer, your pet may be stung by a bee, a wasp, or a hornet. Sometimes dogs also snap at flying insects and in the process are stung in the mouth, on the tongue, or on the lips. If swelling appears in the mouth area, causing difficulty in breathing and swallowing, take it to the veterinarian at once. Do the same thing if allergic problems, such as vomiting, labored breathing, and fits of coughing, occur. You need to examine insect bites on the paw, for example, and, if need be, pull out the insect's stinger. All you need to do is to cool the puncture site with water or ice, unless the dog displays some allergic symptoms.

Eating snow: Most dogs like to romp in the snow, and not infrequently they eat some of it. Diarrhea, stomach aches, and colds can result. Make sure your pet doesn't eat any snow. In addition, never encourage your dog to play by throwing a snowball at it.

On Growing Old and Dying

With appropriate care, small dog breeds on the average have a longer life expectancy than large breeds. Tibetan terriers, for example, are known to be able to live as long as 20 years.

How do we go about transposing dog years into human years? The old calculation—one year of a dog's life = seven years of a human's—is still in circulation, but it is not really accurate. A dog is full-grown at 12 months; it has come of age, so to speak (age 18 for humans). From this point on, we calculate that one dog year is the equivalent of five human years. Thus, a 10-year-old dog corresponds to a 63-year-old human being ($18 + [9 \times 5] = 63$).

With increasing age, after about 12 years, every dog experiences some loss of its keenness of vision and hearing. That bothers a dog less than a human, however. As long as its sense of smell is intact, the dog is scarcely affected, because it is an olfactory (uses its sense of smell) animal by nature. Later on it will move at a slower pace on walks, and it may not remain completely housebroken. Then you simply need to be somewhat more careful with your housemate of many years.

The last goodbye need not be said until your dog is in pain and is beginning to suffer. Let the veterinarian release it from its agony with an injection. It should go without saying that you will make this final trip to the veterinarian together with your pet and not entrust that duty to a friend. After all, the dog has spent its entire life with you and shared your joys and sorrows. As the veterinarian gives your pet the injection, hold it in your arms and stroke it. You owe that to your companion of many years' standing.

The young cairn terrier wants to play with the rottweiler.

Puppies and young dogs generally can get away with a lot in dealing with adult dogs. Nature has inhibited the big dogs' impulse to bite. You need to be careful, however, with overbred dogs that have behavior problems. They will even bite puppies.

Your Dog's Love Life

Before you breed your dog, you need to be aware that raising puppies requires a great deal of know-how, room, time, and money. Naturally, it is a wonderful experience to watch puppies growing up, but your dog's emotional balance does not depend on whether it has sired or given birth to offspring in its life.

Granted, the little offspring of small dog breeds are extremely cute. That fact may quickly inspire in you a desire to have you female dog, or bitch, bred. In addition, you may be influenced by the widespread superstition that a bitch has to have whelped at least once in her life in order to remain emotionally stable. That is untrue, however, as has been proved. Both males that have never mated with a female and bitches that have borne no offspring are happy.

Responsibility for Breeding

Your small dog is a purebred. In order to preserve the positive traits of character and the faultless anatomy of the breed, it is important to use only the "best" dogs for breeding purposes. Consequently, a dog with an officially recognized pedigree has excellent prerequisites for breeding. The ancestors of your dog are listed in its pedigree. An experienced breeder can draw conclusions based on this document, because, of course, the forebears also pass on their characteristics to their descendants.

If you would like to breed your pet, the breeder from whom you bought it is an important person to approach. In addition, you can join a breed club in order to become more knowledgeable. As a member, you will receive a copy of the breeding regulations, which govern the entire formal course of events where breeding is concerned, as well as the necessary provisions for protection of animals. Several legal requirements also apply to breeding, and for information about them it is best to consult the appropriate parent organization of the American Kennel Club, breed club, or your individual state or local breed club.

Before you start to breed your pet, you need to realize that raising dogs requires not only a great deal of money, time, and room, but also an enormous amount of specialized knowledge.

Breeding Regulations

Age: The regulations in Europe are far stricter than in the United States. In most European countries the breeding regulations of each breed club specify the age at which the dogs can first be bred. Accordingly, males normally are permitted to breed once they reach the age of nine months, while bitches should not be mated until they are 15 months old. In the United States if you own a registered dog you may breed it as you please, although "strong suggestions" regarding breeding age are given by the different breed clubs.

Breeding permit: In Europe it is not issued until your dog takes part in a breed show recognized by your club. There, a specialty judge will rule on its suitability for breeding. Only dogs that get a very good score are approved for breeding. No breeding permit is required in the United States.

Breeding intervals: In Europe, the intervals at which a bitch may be bred are set forth. These intervals are determined by the number of puppies she has delivered in each litter. My personal opinion is that bitches should cease to be bred after their seventh year of life. Similar breeding intervals are recommended in the U.S.

The Right Partner for Your Bitch

Your neighbor's male is not always the best partner for your bitch. Often you have to search long and hard for a suitable stud. Ask your dog's breeder and your dog club for advice in making the selection.

Once the right male has been located, you have to take your female to him, because he usually will service females only in his accustomed surroundings. The male's owner will charge a fee for the servicing—or may trade it for one or more puppies of *their* choice.

When the Bitch Is in Season

As a rule, a female dog is in season every six months, beginning between her sixth and eighth months of life. This period of time, also known as estrus or heat, lasts about three weeks, and she is receptive to mating only during this time. In the preliminary phase (proestrus), which lasts about 10 days, her vulva swells and she becomes restless, sometimes moody, and urinates more frequently than usual. Males are already beginning to be attracted to her, but she rejects them with annoyance. Between the third and seventh days of proestrus, a bloody discharge is apparent in the female. At the end of this preliminary phase, the discharge turns glassy pink (tenth to sixteenth days). Now the female is willing to accept the male. That is evident in her habit of immediately moving her tail to the side and standing motionless when you stroke the base of her tail. Drive your bitch to the male's residence on the eleventh day, if possible, and bring her back to him on the thirteenth day to be serviced again, just to be on the safe side.

Mating

During estrus, the bitch remains receptive to mating for several days. When the male and the female are brought together, it may be that the two animals—depending on their temperaments and their liking for one another—first play together before mating takes place. During the mating act, the male's penis enlarges, and at the same time the female's vaginal ring constricts; the dogs are "tied" together. The mating act can last over 30 minutes.

Pregnancy

The gestation period generally is about 63 days in duration. To calculate the probable whelping date, count the days starting with the last date of service. Keep your engagement calendar clear for that time.

If the bitch has conceived, a slight rounding of her little abdomen will become apparent after the fifth week. Her behavior is calmer, and she frequently is more affectionate than usual. Plenty of outdoor exercise now will do her good, provided she is not overtaxed. Also, keep her from climbing stairs and jumping down off the armchair or the couch.

The diet of a pregnant bitch has to be higher in vitamins and more

These Italian greyhound puppies are now four weeks old, and their mother suckles them only in a standing position.

nutritious than in "normal times." For that reason, from the fifth week on, mix wheat germ, calcium supplements, and bone meal with her dog food. The amount of food may be doubled, and it should be divided into two or three meals per day. The female's liquid intake increases during pregnancy, and she needs to have fresh water available at all times.

False Pregnancy

Twenty to 30 percent of all bitches suffer from a condition known as false pregnancy, or pseudopregnancy. Usually those affected are either older animals or very young ones that have not whelped yet. The symptoms are identical to those of true pregnancy. The bitch's girth increases, she starts to build a "nest," her nipples swell, and she is restless. As a "baby substitute" she may choose a toy or a stuffed doll—or even a rolled sock—for example. She even secretes milk to suckle the imaginary puppy. Take the puppy substitute away from your pet. I have had good experience with cold vinegar compresses, which I placed on my dog's teats three times a day. The vinegar water reduces the swelling in them.

Tip: If the teats become inflamed, you need to take your bitch to the veterinarian.

Preparations for Whelping

The whelping box: The size of the whelping box depends on the size of the dog breed (example: for a Yorkshire terrier, a box 32 inches [80 cm] long, 20 inches [50 cm] wide, and 12 inches [30 cm] high is sufficient). Ideally, on one of the long sides the box should have a little door that can be latched or, alternatively, an indentation. That will allow the female to leave the box easily, and it will also keep the little pups from tumbling out. Inside the box, on three sides, attach

This Yorkie puppy peers adventurously out of its little basket.

round wood about 2.4 inches (6 cm) above the bottom of the box and 1.6 inches (4 cm) from the side walls. This will create spaces into which the newborns can retreat if their mother rolls too far over on her side and threatens to crush the little creatures. Spread newspaper and fresh towels on the bottom of the box.

Put the box in a quiet room with a temperature of about 64.4°F (18°C), and let the bitch start sleeping in it several weeks before her whelping date.

Things to do before the whelping: The bitch needs to be wormed about four weeks before she whelps (see page 52). Approximately two weeks before the estimated whelping date, make sure that the veterinarian can be reached if an emergency arises. About one or two days before the whelping, disinfect the whelping box and its surroundings. Clip away any long hair on the mother dog's abdomen to let the little puppies reach her teats easily later on. With long-haired dogs, the body hair has to be tied up; otherwise, newborn pups can get caught in it and even be strangled.

Finally, place the following at hand for your use: clean towels, string, a suitable pair of scissors for severing the umbilical cord, a spray disinfectant, a thermometer, and a scale.

Whelping

Phase 1: About 24 to 36 hours before giving birth, the bitch's body temperature drops to 98.6°F (37°C). It will not return to normal (see page 54) until just before the delivery. The day the dog whelps, she is restless, lying down in one corner after another. The preparatory uterine contractions have begun. Let her run around in the whelping room, as exercise can make her labor easier.

Phase 2: Now the next stage of labor, which entails bearing down to open the mouth of the womb, begins.

These two poodles were brought together for the purpose of mating.

In dogs, the act of mating sometimes lasts up to an hour. Never attempt to separate two dogs with force. Both animals could be seriously injured.

The dog will either stand or lie on her side, while the contractions come at increasingly short intervals. Liquid is discharged from the vagina, and soon thereafter the first puppy appears, surrounded by the fetal membrane and the ring-shaped placenta. The dog eats the fetal membrane and placenta, biting through the umbilical cord in the process. Then she licks the newborn with her tongue to stimulate its circulation.

Sometimes the female is too exhausted or already busy delivering the next puppy, so that you need to intervene:

• To clear the puppy's respiratory passages quickly, tear open the fetal membrane near the newborn's nose and clean its head and muzzle. Use your finger to remove any mucus from the puppy's mouth cavity.

• Next, briskly rub the little dog dry with a towel.

• The first whimper is the indication that the puppy has enough air. Now you can place it near its mother's teats, to which it normally crawls on its own.

• If the mother should fail to sever the umbilical cord herself, tie it off tightly with string, close to the puppy's belly. Then cut through the cord about .4 inch (1 cm) above the spot where it is tied. The remaining portion of the umbilical cord will dry up and subsequently fall off.

Tip: After the whelping, make sure there is a constant level of warmth in the whelping box. One good method is to attach an infrared heat bulb (150 watts) about 50 inches (1.30 m) above the whelping box.

Complications: Particularly with small dog breeds, complications during whelping are not uncommon, for a variety of reasons. At times, despite the uterine contractions, no puppy is expelled. Sometimes the fetal membrane breaks in the birth canal, and the puppy gets stuck. Occasionally a puppy doesn't breathe properly just after birth. It would be pointless to give first-aid instructions here. If something goes amiss, I recommend that you notify your veterinarian at once.

Development of the Puppies

Baby dogs are born with a full coat of hair. They are blind until they are 10 days old, and they cannot hear until the twelfth day. On the other hand, their sense of smell begins to function at the very start, and it helps them locate the source of milk at their mother's teats every time, without fail.

About the tenth day after the whelping, you should begin gradually lowering the temperature in the whelping room, to get the little animals used to normal room temperature.

The puppies spend the first three weeks right at their mother's side, and they sleep a great deal.

After about the fourth week the puppies first venture outside the whelping box to explore.

At the age of six weeks they are weaned and need solid food (see below). This is the beginning of their most important stage, the so-called imprinting phase. The puppies gradually "discover" themselves, their siblings, and human beings. Spend plenty of time with the little dogs now, so that they have close contact with humans. Later on, they will trust people and behave in an open manner.

In the eighth to twelfth week the puppies learn to distinguish between play and earnest. They try out their social behavior by tussling with their siblings, and they practice various other modes of behavior. Behavioral scientists have coined the term "socialization phase" for this stage of development.

Feeding the Puppies

The mother dog, or dam, can take care of her puppies completely on her own for about the first four weeks after she has whelped. During this time she continues to need twice her usual amount of food. Suckling her offspring results in calcium loss, which you need to offset by adding a daily dose of calcium to your bitch's main meal.

After that time, you need to relieve her of some of her burden by serving the puppies additional food two or three times a day. I highly recommend the commercially available puppy rations. I also have had good experience with pureed baby food: beef, veal, or chicken mixed with vegetables. Enrich the meal by adding a vitamin and calcium supplement daily (see Feeding and Nutrition, page 45).

After the sixth week of life the puppies are completely weaned and should be given four to five meals per day. I use a commercial puppy food.

This burglar-proof grid can be inserted easily into a car window. In this way, the dog is ensured of a constant supply of fresh air whenever it has to wait in the car.

Portraits of Popular Small Dog Breeds

Description, Health Care, and Comments

In the portrait section that follows, 36 popular small dogs are presented, from the affenpinscher to the toy spitz (Pomeranian). Within the individual profiles, the information is broken down as follows:

• Introduction: Here you will find information on the breed's place of origin, if known, and the crossbreeding that resulted in this breed.

• Size and weight: The height of the dog at the withers and its weight are given, based on the breed standard (see page 4).

• Coat and color: The texture of the coat of hair is described, along with the color varieties permitted by the breed standard.

• Temperament: I have summarized the typical traits of character of the breed in question, in order to give you additional help in selecting a breed.

• Grooming: Pointers on coat maintenance, based on actual experience.

• Care: Information on the amount of living space and exercise the dog requires.

• Breed-related problems: This category deals with the diseases that typically occur in a breed and with anomalies such as patellar dislocation (slipping kneecap). The tendency to develop dislocation of the kneecap is hereditary, and this problem affects many small dogs, such as papillons, Yorkshire terriers, and Chihuahuas, for example. Responsible breeders, however, are constantly trying to improve the breed quality.

• Comments: Any peculiarities of the breed are pointed out.

The Right Dog Breed for You

Most people are already envisioning the "purebred of their dreams" by the time they have decided to acquire a dog. Often they consider only the dog's external appearance. You should not be guided by that alone, however. Choose your pet on the basis of the circumstances in which you live and your personality.

Take the Chihuahua, for example, for which, because of its diminutive stature, there is room in even the tiniest apartment. You don't need to take it for long walks. The main thing is that it get enough exercise. For older people who are no longer good walkers or people who don't enjoy lengthy walks, a Chihuahua is precisely the right companion. Miniature poodles and toy poodles, too, can be kept in small apartments, but these very high-spirited dogs need substantially more exercise outdoors than Chihuahuas. In addition, poodles have to be trimmed regularly, and that can be expensive. Some dogs have trouble climbing stairs. If you live on an upper floor of an apartment building that has no elevator, you have to carry your pet. Since a dachshund can weigh up to 20 pounds (9 kg), that may become a problem for children and older people. If you are a fairly quiet person by nature, you are ill-advised to buy a lively, bold spitz. You are better off with a Maltese or a pug.

Before you decide on a dog breed, you need to gather information about the breed's character traits and the care it needs. Only people who are fully aware of those things before purchasing a dog will be able to show adequate patience and understanding for their new housemate later on.

Affenpinscher

1. The wire-haired, intrepid affenpinscher can be kept in even the tiniest apartment if it gets enough exercise outdoors.

1. The affenpinscher was first bred in Germany.

1. Affenpinscher

The smallest member of the family of pinschers and schnauzers, the affenpinscher originated in Germany.

It enjoyed great popularity between the First and Second World Wars. An impish miniature that proved itself as a catcher of rats and mice and was also used on quail and rabbits.

Appearance: A wreath of hair frames its round little face with its prominent forehead. The muzzle is short, but not upturned as in the miniature griffon. Its teeth often protrude somewhat. The eyes are round.

It has bushy, bristly eyebrows and erect, pointed ears. Its body is stocky and compact.

Size and weight: Height at the withers, up to 12 inches (30 cm); weight, 6.6 to 8.8 pounds (3–4 kg).

Coat and color: The affenpinscher has a dense coat, which is hard, lusterless, and shaggy. White markings are considered faults. A slight gray or brown hue is not penalized.

Temperament: It can be bright and full of life, but occasionally also placid. Lovable, inclined to play jokes, and truly devoted. It is very attached to its home. Despite its diminutive

stature, it makes a good watchdog.

Grooming: Daily combing and brushing are enough. Bathe only when absolutely necessary. The affenpinscher needs to be trimmed periodically to maintain its typical appearance.

Care: If it gets enough exercise outdoors, it can be kept even in an extremely small apartment.

Breed-related problems: Mobility problems due to overly "steep" hindquarters.

Bichon Frisé

2. These two bichon frisés are romping exuberantly in a meadow.

2. Bichon Frisé

Portraits from past centuries provide the evidence that there was a bichon in almost every aristocratic household of France and Italy. As its mistress's constant companion, the bichon was responsible for seeing to it that she passed the day in good spirits. Then at night the dog had to serve as her bed-warmer.

Appearance: The dense, abundant coat makes this dog's appearance unmistakable. Round, dark eyes and a black nose are the only points of contrast on the light-colored head, which seems outsized because of the coat of hair. Under its coat is concealed an anatomically correct body structure.

Size and weight: Height at the withers, 11 to 12 inches (25–30 cm); weight, 11 to 15.4 pounds (5–7 kg).

Coat and color: Fine, silky hair; very thick and curled in loose corkscrews. In an adult dog, the hair is about 3 to 4 inches (7-10 cm) long. The only color is pure white; the breed standard deems the presence of colored markings to be a fault.

Temperament: Full of charm, intelligence, and merriment. Aggressiveness toward humans and other dogs is foreign to its nature.

Grooming: If the bichon is to retain its good looks, it needs to be brushed daily and bathed as necessary. Clean the eyes and eyelids daily, to keep the flow of tears from discoloring the hair. Cut the ends of the coat to reveal the natural outline of the body.

Care: Because of its anatomy, the bichon frisé is a small dog that loves exercise. Relatively long walks and hikes are no problem for it, with proper training. Nevertheless, it is quite content in an apartment.

Bolognese, Boston Terrier

1. Bolognese tend to be quiet, serious dogs.

2. These three Boston terriers look altogether dashing.

Size and weight: Height at the withers, 10 to 12 inches (25–30 cm); weight, about 5 to 9 pounds (2.5–4 kg).

Coat and color: The coat of hair is long and fluffy, and it covers the body uniformly. Only at the front of the face is it somewhat shorter. The hair must be pure white in color, with no colored markings.

Temperament: Serious and reserved. It tends to be distant with strangers, but is truly devoted to its owner. In familiar surroundings, it moves with restrained animation and tends to behave in a subdued manner.

Grooming: Brush daily. Make sure you don't brush and comb too hard or the hair will lose its fluffy curls. The eyes have to be cleaned every day.

Care: Its quiet demeanor makes it suitable for people who don't want an overly high-spirited dog. Ideal pet for apartment dwellers.

2. Boston Terrier

The result of a cross between English bulldogs and white English terriers, the breed was officially recognized in the United States in 1893.

Appearance: The round head with its blocky muzzle is reminiscent of a bulldog. The proud attitude and athletic body were inherited from the terriers. An imposing dog whose appearance depends heavily on the distribution of the colors.

Size and weight: Height at the withers, 12 to 15 inches (30–38 cm); weight, about 13 to 24 pounds (6–11 kg).

1. Bolognese

The city of Bologna (Italy) probably gave its name to this bichon variety (bichon bolognais). Even in paintings from the Middle Ages one can see small dogs with the typical Bolognese hair.

Appearance: Slightly bristled, fluffy coat of hair. Round, dark eyes with an intelligent look and a large, black nose determine the facial expression. Square body with level back line. The tail is carried rolled up on the back.

Cairn Terrier

Coat and color: The coat of hair is short, smooth, glossy, and fine-textured. The color can be brindle with white markings or black with white markings. Its value and breeding potential are greatly lessened if the head is not evenly marked and if both eyes are not in the black area.

Temperament: Its temperament calls for consistency in training. Fear is alien to its nature, as is aggressive behavior toward humans. With other dogs, however, it is ready to get into a fight.

Grooming: With a damp cloth, remove any hair that has been shed; clean the large eyes every day. Cut the nails from time to time.

Care: An athletic dog that needs an athletically inclined owner. The Boston terrier's muscles have to be exercised. A daily walk is compulsory.

Breed-related problems: Dislocation of the kneecap.

3. *The cairn terrier once was used for hunting.*

3. Cairn Terrier

Its place of origin is western Scotland. There, while hunting foxes, badgers, and other vermin, it had to prove that it possessed courage and perseverance.

Appearance: At first glance, it should look shaggy and unsophisticated. Cheeky look in its eye. Its body is bursting with energy.

Size and weight: Height at the withers, 11 to 12 inches (28–31 cm); weight, 16 pounds (7.5 kg).

Coat and color: Double coat of hair with thick, soft undercoat and harsh, longer outer coat that protects it from all kinds of weather. Most common colors: red, gray, sand-colored or wheat-colored with black tips. Objectionable: black, white, blackish brown.

Temperament: On the one hand, this dog is a bundle of energy, undaunted by hustle and bustle or by large families, however many children they include. On the other hand, the cairn terrier can be affectionate and fond of cuddling. Its urge to hunt is still present, however, and you need to train it firmly and maintain your authority over it.

Grooming: Its coat of hair is supposed to look unsophisticated and natural, but regular brushing and combing still are necessary, as well as plucking out the dead hairs with a trimming knife.

Cavalier King Charles Spaniel, King Charles Spaniel

2. The King Charles spaniel, in comparison with the cavalier King Charles spaniel, has a shorter muzzle.

1. Cavalier King Charles spaniel with puppy.

1. Cavalier King Charles Spaniel

This small spaniel had spaniel-like hunting dogs as ancestors. It soon became the favorite of many royal and princely households, but by the beginning of the twentieth century the breed had become almost extinct.

Appearance: Upper part of the head flat, eyes large; fringed, drooping ears. The tail should not be carried over the back.

Size and weight: Height at the withers, 12 to 14 inches (30–35 cm); weight, about 12 to 18 pounds (5.5–8.5 kg).

Coat and color: Long, silky coat of hair free from curl; slight waviness is permissible. Four color varieties: white with chestnut-red patches (Blenheim); white with black patches and tan markings (tricolor or Prince Charles); black with tan markings on the head and tail (black-and-tan); solid red (ruby).

Temperament: Fearless, lively, athletic, and cheerful. Very fond of children.

Grooming: Daily brushing and combing. Bathe as needed. Regular ear and eye care.

Keeping: Can be kept even in a small apartment, provided it can let off steam on walks.

2. King Charles Spaniel

During the reigns of King Charles I and King Charles II in England, the short-nosed English toy spaniel, or "King Charles spaniel," was extremely popular—hence its name.

Appearance: Prominently domed skull, ears set low on head, markedly pushed-back nose; as a rule, docked tail.

Weight and size: Height at the withers, up to 12 inches (30 cm); weight, 6.6 to 13 pounds (3–6 kg).

Coat and color: Silky coat; particularly profuse on the ears and legs. Four color varieties (see cavalier King Charles spaniel).

Chihuahua

3. Chihuahuas are the "half-pints" among the small dog breeds. There are some that weigh only 17.6 ounces (500 g). Such "minis" may have a limited life expectancy.

3. Short-haired and long-haired Chihuahuas.

Temperament: Quiet, placid, introverted. Very reserved with strangers. Runs away from other dogs.

Grooming: Brush and comb regularly. Clean eyes and ears daily.

Care: An apartment dog. Fairly long walks possible with proper training.

3. Chihuahua

Believed to be indigenous to Mexico.

Appearance: The original breed has short hair. The long-haired variety was created by crossbreeding with small spitzes and papillons. Pronounced apple-shaped head with large eyes and ears.

Size and weight: Height at the withers, about 8 inches (20 cm); weight, 2.2 to 6.6 pounds (1–3 kg).

Color and coat: The short-haired (smooth-coated) Chihuahua has a glossy, close-fitting coat. The long-coated variety has long, silky hair. It has a ruff, "pants" on its hind legs, and long hair on its tail.

Temperament: Affectionate and protective. Very courageous, even when dealing with large dogs. Reserved with strangers.

Grooming: Groom the smooth-coated Chihuahua's coat with a damp cloth. The silky hair of the long-coated Chihuahua needs to be brushed and bathed regularly.

Care: Even the tiniest apartment has enough room. One walk daily is sufficient. The dog can even get used to a cat litter box. Not a "toy" for children.

Breed-related problems: In very tiny animals of this breed, an open cranium. Incomplete set of teeth, early loss of teeth. Dislocation of kneecap.

Chinese Crested Hairless

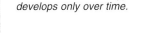

1. At first, the puppies still have a full head of hair. The typical mane develops only over time.

1. Owning a Chinese crested hairless is definitely a matter of individual taste.

1. Chinese Crested Hairless

2. Chinese Crested Powderpuff

The Chinese crested hairless is one of the rarest and most exotic of all the unusual dog breeds.

The history of this breed's origin goes far back to prehistoric times and is in part obscure. Millennia ago, in Africa, a hairless dog—the so-called *Canis africanus*—arose from a mutation (alteration in a gene or chromosome). From Africa this dog traveled to China and from there in turn to America, on board tea clippers.

Chinese crested hairless dogs have one gene for hairlessness and one for the development of a complete coat of hair. That is why their litters always include some dogs with a full coat, which are known as "powderpuffs."

Appearance: A lively, graceful dog with a narrow muzzle, the Chinese crested has a fine-boned skeleton.

Its skin, which is pleasantly soft and warm to the touch, ranges from pink to dark brown in color. It may also be spotted.

The hair on its head may resemble a horse's flowing mane or, on the other hand, it may stand up like a "punker hairdo." The hair at the end of the tail is reminiscent of a plume, while that on its feet looks like little socks.

The powderpuff has long, soft hair covering its entire body. At first glance you might mistake it for a dwarf Afghan hound.

Weight and size: Height at the withers, 9 to 11 inches (23–33 cm); weight, up to 12 pounds (5.5 kg).

Coat and color: Any color or combination of colors is permissible.

While the Chinese crested hairless has hair only on its

Chinese Crested Powderpuff

head, at the tip of its tail, and on its feet, the powderpuff's coat of hair consists of a long, soft top coat with an undercoat.

Temperament: The breed has a boundless need for affection. Its paws, which resemble hare's feet, can embrace you tenderly. Many dogs follow their owners' every step, and they are extremely timid with strangers. This is the dog for people capable of providing copious amounts of affection at all times. If you want a faithful companion who wishes to be at your side and nowhere else, look no further.

Grooming: The hair-covered parts of the hairless dog have to be brushed once a day. From time to time it needs a bath and an application of skin-care lotion.

The powderpuff requires the same time-consuming hair care as any other long-haired dog, because the woolly undercoat quickly becomes matted.

Care: It is an ideal apartment dog, but it also needs plenty of exercise outdoors. Short outings in winter are no problem for your pet, if you dry it thoroughly afterward. In summer there is a risk of sunburn, however, because it dearly loves to lie out in the blazing sun. A good sunscreen and only short stays outdoors are advisable. The sun also has an intensifying effect on the skin color, which sometimes turns almost black. Chinese cresteds with spotted skin, in particular, have to be protected from overexposure to sun.

The hairless dogs are hearty eaters, as they need plenty of

2. The hairy version of the Chinese crested hairless dog is the Chinese crested powderpuff.

energy for increased production of heat.

In addition, they are ideal pets for people who are allergic to dog hair.

Breed-related problems: Particularly with Chinese cresteds that have a very fine-structured build, you need to make sure that they do not jump too far or too high (they are good climbers).

They usually do not have a complete set of teeth, and in addition, they lose their second set of teeth much faster than other dogs.

Dislocation of the kneecap is a common problem.

Comments: Because of its appearance, the Chinese crested will always remain a rarity, which is just as well. You need to think very carefully about the acquisition of such a dog, because the animal may not easily adjust to a new home.

Cotón de Tulear

1. The cotón de Tulear is a decidedly lovable dog.

1. Cotón de Tulear

The island of Madagascar in the Indian Ocean is the home of this bichon variety. The breed gained official recognition in 1970.

Appearance: The cottony coat of hair determines this small dog's appearance. The head is defined by the slight stop, the dark, lively eyes, and the well-developed muzzle with the dark nose.

The line of the back should be slightly arched; the tail is carried over the back.

Size and weight: Height at the withers: males, up to 12.6 inches (32 cm), females, 11 inches (28 cm); weight, about 7 to 9 pounds (3.5–4 kg).

Coat and color: Fine-textured coat. The slightly wavy coat of hair, about 3 inches (8 cm) in length, has a cottony look. The color is white with bisque-colored (pinkish tan) or slightly darker patches, primarily on the ears.

Temperament: Breed fanciers claim that it possesses all the good qualities desirable in a dog. It is perpetually in good spirits and, if kept as a family pet, provides entertainment. It is loyal, intelligent, and dynamic.

Grooming: Regular brushing and bathing contribute to the coton's well-groomed appearance, as does cleaning of the eyelids. After your pet has eaten, clean its beard hair.

Care: The coton is a typical apartment dog. Its original utilization for hunting (mainly to get rid of unpleasant small rodents in the vicinity of human settlements) no longer plays any part in its keeping.

Breed-related problems: Because the history of the cotón de Tulear breed is so brief, practical information still has to be collected and evaluated.

2. Dachshund

The dachshund, also known as the badger dog or sausage dog, developed from the dachshund-like but long-legged breed of hounds (braques). As early as the late seventeenth century, "badger-crawlers" were mentioned in the relevant literature. Originally it was employed only as a hunting dog, but today it is predominantly a family pet.

Appearance: Elongated, but sturdy figure with strong muscles.

A challenging, jaunty way of holding its head.

An intelligent facial expression is obligatory.

Despite the shortness of the limbs in relation to the long body, it should not appear deformed, ungainly, or limited in mobility.

Size and weight: The size is stated in terms of the chest circumference. The standard dachshund weighs from 11 to 20 pounds (5–9 kg) and has a

Dachshund

chest circumference of more than 14 inches (35 cm).

The miniature dachshund weighs 6.6 to 11 pounds (3–5 kg), with a chest measuring 12 to 14 inches (30–35 cm) around.

The "rabbit dachshund" may weigh up to 6.6 pounds (3 kg), with a chest measurement of up to 12 inches (30 cm).

Coat and color: The short-haired or smooth dachshund has a thick, close-fitting coat of hair; the wire-haired dachshund has rough hair with a thick undercoat.

The long-haired dachshund must have a silky, soft coat of long hair, with long hair hanging from the backs of the legs and from the tail.

For short- and long-haired dachshunds, the most common colors are red (tan) and black with red markings. The wire-haired dogs come in all shades of wild boar (brindle).

Temperament: This dog may be a comedian and an individualist, but at any rate it is intelligent and adaptable. If it is well trained, it will obey.

Grooming: For the easy-upkeep of smooth dachshunds, occasionally brushing the coat and wiping it clean with a damp cloth are sufficient.

The high-maintenance long-haired dachshund has to be brushed and combed daily, to keep the silky hair from becoming matted.

The wire-haired dachshund needs to be trimmed from time to time.

Care: An apartment that can be reached by elevator is no problem for a dachshund, if it

2. *Miniature dachshunds have extremely short legs.*

2. *Long-haired dachshunds are known for their silky-soft coats.*

gets outdoor exercise regularly. Its need for activity, especially while young, is great.

Breed-related problems: "Dachshund paralysis," due to intervertebral disk degeneration and spinal cord injury, is a hereditary disease.

With increasing age, make certain that the dog's weight stays in a healthy range.

Miniature Griffon

1. Griffons always look a little ill-humored, although they are more apt to be friendly and affectionate by nature. Their crossbreeding with Pekingese is evident in their facial expression.

1. The Brussels griffon has a rough, fox-red coat.

1. Miniature Griffon

This Belgian breed of toy dogs, with which the pug was used as a cross, occurs in three varieties: the Brussels griffon, the Belgian griffon, and the Brabant griffon (petit brabançon). They are distinguished by their colors and coats of hair. The breed was quite popular in Belgium as early as the end of the nineteenth century.

Appearance: Large, round head with ears carried erect or semierect; very large, round eyes; short muzzle with distinctly protruding chin and protrusive occlusion.

The square body with the level back and powerful chest are carried on straight, strong-boned legs.

Size and weight: Height at the withers, up to 12.6 inches (32 cm); weight, depending on size, 4.4 to 11 pounds (2–5 kg).

Coat and color: The Brussels griffon has a hard, shaggy, medium-length, dense coat of fox-colored hair.

The hair of the Belgian griffon is identical in texture and length to that of the Brussels variety. Its color, however, is black; also black with red-brown grizzling.

The Brabant griffon's coat of hair, by comparison, is short and thick; its colors are red or black with reddish markings. The black mask is reminiscent of the crossbred pug.

Temperament: Griffons are extremely devoted to their owners. In their accustomed environment they are high-spirited, lively, and very alert. They adapt to their family and get along well with other dogs.

With strange humans they tend to be reserved and cautious.

Grooming: For the long-haired varieties, regular brushing and combing are necessary. Light trimming can improve the dog's appearance. The large eyes have to be

74

Havanese

cleaned daily, as well as the folds of skin around the nose, to prevent inflammations or infestation by mites.

Care: Because griffons bark little and not loudly, they are well suited as apartment dogs. They like to run and romp about, and they have a long life expectancy (around 15 years). Hot or humid weather causes problems for these short-nosed dogs. They tend to snore.

Breed-related problems: Large puppies, which make the whelping process exhausting and often require cesarian delivery.

2. *Its coat of hair is the trademark of the Havanese.*

2. Havanese

This dog belongs to the bichon group. The first bichons probably came from the Mediterranean area to the Caribbean on merchant vessels. They continued to be bred on the island of Cuba. Over the centuries, they developed into a separate breed, the Havanese, or bichon havanais.

In 1963 the Havanese breed was given official recognition.

Appearance: The head is characterized by its flat, broad upper part, drop ears, large, dark eyes, and prominent muzzle.

The body is longer than it is tall. The tail, which is covered with long, soft hair, is carried over the back in the form of a bishop's staff.

Size and weight: Height at the withers, 14 inches (36 cm); weight, not exceeding 13 pounds (6 kg).

Coat and color: The soft coat of hair is loose and fluffy. It forms strands that end in a slight curl.

The color is rarely pure white; dark beige, yellow-brown, and tobacco brown are quite common. Gray shades also occur.

Temperament: The Havanese is always cheerful and in a good mood. Aggressiveness toward humans and other dogs is alien to its friendly, but unobtrusive manner of behavior.

Grooming: The hair has to be regularly brushed the wrong way; when the Havanese shakes itself after being brushed, the hair will fall back into the desired position and produce the typical outward image.

Care: The Havanese can be kept in an apartment if it is allowed to indulge its unmistakable desire to be in motion by taking lengthy walks each day.

Breed-related problems: The breed standard is not yet established. In addition to very petite animals, there are also very robust ones.

Japanese Chin, Lhasa Apso

1. The Japanese Chin can be very unforgiving.

2. The Lhasa apso is an extremely frolicsome dog.

1. Japanese Chin

The origin of the breed has not been determined. The first dogs of this kind are said to have come from China to Japan hundreds of years ago. They were kept and bred at the Japanese imperial court.

Appearance: The head is round and domed, and appears large for the size of the dog. The ears are flat and lie close to the head. Round, dark eyes that protrude slightly and are set wide apart. The bridge of the nose is very short; the jaw is broad and prominent. Short, square body with wide chest. The forelegs are raised high when the dog walks.

Size and weight: Height at the withers, 7 to 11 inches (18–28 cm); weight, up to 9 pounds (4 kg).

Coat and color: Silky, soft coat of hair. Profuse hair on the body but scantier on the head. White ground color, black patches on the body, evenly distributed black marking on the head.

Temperament: Cheerful, watchful, and receptive. It is sensitive and becomes insulted if it feels it is being wrongly treated. Peaceable toward other dogs. Reserved with strangers.

Grooming: Regular brushing and combing gives the coat a silky luster. Clean eyes daily. Clean the drooping ears regularly.

Care: Even the tiniest apartment has room enough, but the Japanese Chin needs a walk every day.

2. Lhasa Apso

This breed originated in Tibet. Lhasa apsos were bred in the monasteries as well as in the palace of the Dalai Lama. After World War I, some of these dogs came to England and the United States.

Appearance: The profusion of hair conceals a healthy body structure. The hidden eyes are medium-sized and dark. Long body, well ribbed up. The legs are straight and well developed. The tail is carried over the back.

Petit Chien Lion (Löwchen)

Size and weight: Height at the withers, 10 to 11 inches (25.5–28 cm); weight, undetermined.

Coat and color: The double coat of hair consists of a fine undercoat and a stronger, ground-length outer coat, which should be neither woolly nor silky. All colors are acceptable. The color of a puppy often changes as it grows older.

Temperament: Affectionate, cheerful. It feels happy in its family. It has the qualities of a watchdog, but without being a yapper. In dealing with strangers, it is proud, cautious, and reserved.

Grooming: Daily brushing and combing is essential. Clean the concealed eyes regularly; remove any food remnants from its beard after eating.

Care: The Lhasa apso has a pronounced desire for exercise. Walks are obligatory. Then the dog will be content even in a small apartment.

3. The clip produces the typical outward appearance of the petit chien lion.

3. Petit Chien Lion (Löwchen)

This little dog is often seen in sixteenth-century paintings. It was the companion of aristocratic ladies and gentlemen as well as bishops. Then the breed fell into complete obscurity. A Belgian breeder reestablished breeding after World War II.

Appearance: The classic poodle cut gives the petit chien lion, or little lion dog, its unmistakable appearance. The ears droop. The eyes are large, round, and dark. Short and very muscular body; straight legs. The tail is carried over the back.

Size and weight: Height at the withers, 8 to 15 inches (20–35 cm); weight, about 9 to 15 pounds (4–7 kg).

Coat and color: The coat of hair is fairly long and wavy, but never curly. All colors are acceptable. White, black, gray, and lemon-yellow are most common.

Temperament: High-spirited, very intelligent, and extremely affectionate. Tends to be reserved with strangers. Firm training is called for.

Grooming: Brush and wash regularly. Clip to emphasize the resemblance to a lion: shear about two-thirds of the hair on the body; on the tail, leave about one-fourth; on the legs, leave a bracelet of hair; on the face and muzzle, leave only a beard remaining.

Care: Not a dog for homebodies. Pronounced urge to run and play. Contented even in small apartments, if it gets enough exercise outdoors.

Maltese, Manchester Terrier

1. The Maltese's silky, white coat of hair requires elaborate, time-consuming care. To make matters worse for their owners, Maltese adore romping about wildly—without any regard for the coat you have just put into shape.

2. Manchester terriers look elegant.

1. Maltese

From antiquity well into modern times, it was the companion of elegant, fashionable ladies. Even today it is more of an indoor pet than a dog to take on extended walks.

Appearance: The head is marked by dark, oval eyes and a black nose. Heavily fringed, close-fitting ears. The tail is carried over the back.

Size and weight: Height at the withers, 8 to 10 inches (20–25 cm); weight, 6.6 to 9 pounds (3–4 kg).

Coat and color: The coat of hair is silky; it is long and smooth over the entire body.

Pure white in color.

Temperament: Even-tempered. The Maltese is intelligent, affectionate, fond of children, and easy to train; it tends to be reserved with strangers.

Grooming: Brush and comb daily; bathe regularly. Clean the eyes daily to prevent unsightly tear stains. Remove leftover food from the beard.

Care: The Maltese loves to be in motion. Keeping one in an apartment is not difficult, provided it is walked regularly.

Breed-related problems: Heavy flow of tears, dislocated elbows, cottony coat of hair.

2. Manchester Terrier

This breed—also known as the black-and-tan terrier—originated in the industrial regions of northern England. It was employed for hunting small animals.

Appearance: Smooth-coated, elegant dog. Wedge-shaped head with almond-shaped eyes; ears fall forward; undocked tail.

Size and weight: Height at the withers, 15 to 16.5 inches (40–42 cm) (not precisely a small dog any longer); weight, 17 to 22 pounds (8–10 kg).

Coat and color: Short, smooth coat of hair. Black ground color, mahogany-colored markings on the head, chest, and legs.

Pugs

3. Pugs are not everybody's cup of tea, but they are friendly, lovable dogs.

Temperament: It is high-spirited, vigilant, and friendly with children. When it encounters strangers, it is mistrustful but never aggressive.

Grooming: With a brush and a damp cloth, remove loose hairs shed from the coat. Clean the eyes and ears regularly.

Care: With plentiful exercise on a daily basis, it is suitable also for city apartments. Needs consistency in training.

3. Pug

The breed is indigenous to China. Merchant ships brought the first pugs to Holland around 1400; from there they spread throughout Europe.

Appearance: Stocky body. Deep wrinkles on the face and forehead. Short, broad muzzle with a black mask. Huge, dark eyes. The ears tilt forward. The tail lies in a double curl on the back.

Size and weight: Height at the withers, 10 to 12.6 inches (25–32 cm); weight, about 14 to 18 pounds (6.5–8.5 kg).

Coat and color: Smooth-fitting coat. Ground color: black, silvery gray, yellowish brown to whitish yellow.

Temperament: Very affectionate and desirous of human contact. Unforgiving if unjustly treated. Pleasant temperament.

Grooming: Clean facial creases regularly. Use a brush and a damp cloth to remove loose hairs from the coat.

Care: If you walk it regularly, it will be content in even the tiniest apartment.

Breed-related problems: Heavy breathing in hot, humid weather. Inflammations in the skin folds. Injuries to the large and prominent eyes.

Papillon

1. The origin of the term "papillon" is fairly obvious. The dog got its name from its long-haired ears, which are reminiscent of butterfly wings.

1. Papillons are very self-assured dogs.

1. Papillon

2. Phalène

There are two varieties of the Continental toy spaniel: the papillon and the phalène. They can be distinguished only by their ears: The papillon has erect ears, while the phalène—the original form—has drooping, close-fitting ears. Otherwise, they are identical in appearance.

As early as the twelfth century, toy spaniels were popular among the aristocratic ladies of the Spanish court. In the fourteenth and fifteenth centuries, they were to be found in almost every noble household in Europe. One prominent admirer of these dogs was King Henry III of France (1551–1589). Their fanciers also included the Austrian Empress Maria Theresa and her daughter Marie Antoinette.

Famous masters such as Titian, Rubens, and Jan Vermeer included toy spaniels in many of their paintings. During the French Revolution, however, these dogs were almost wiped out.

The erect-eared papillon did not come into being until the nineteenth century, as the result of crossbreeding with the spitz and the Chihuahua. Its ears, which are opened like the wings of a butterfly, earned it the name papillon, or "butterfly dog." It gained popularity very rapidly, and now the phalène, also called the "moth," is rarely to be found.

The papillon and the phalène are very intelligent dogs and have a robust constitution. With good care, they can live to an age of 17 years.

Appearance: The heavily fringed ears, the dark, almond-shaped eyes, and the muzzle that tapers to a point give the toy spaniel its unmistakable jaunty appearance.

Phalène

The body is long rather than tall, and the legs are fine-boned and straight. The tail is set high and has long feathering. It is carried in an arch above the back.

Size and weight: In these small spaniels, the height at the withers should not exceed 11 inches (28 cm).

Their weight must be at least 3 pounds (1.5 kg), and it may not exceed 10 pounds (4.5 kg) in males and 11 pounds (5 kg) in females.

Coat and color: The profuse coat of fine hair has a slight wave. There should be no undercoat. The hair is long and abundant on the ears, tail, and backs of the legs. The head is covered with short, smooth hair.

All colors are permissible. The most common is a white ground color with black or red markings. Self-colored dogs— solid red, brown, or black— rarely occur.

Temperament: The papillon and the phalène are saucy, charming, and self-assured. Their qualities also include a natural gaiety and intelligence, in combination with great vivacity.

As apartment pets, these dogs, which enjoy human contact, are easy to train and affectionate. They adapt very readily to their family. They must not be thought of as "children's toys," however.

From the very beginning of the training process, you need to work on the dog's inborn tendency to fervent barking.

Grooming: You should brush and comb the papillon and the phalène daily. That is essential

2. The phalène's drooping ears distinguish it from the papillon.

if the coat of hair is to acquire the desired luster.

The ears and eyes also have to be cleaned thoroughly at regular intervals (see How-to pages 42 and 43).

Care: The papillon and the phalène are content everywhere—in an apartment or a house, in the city or out in the country.

They love exercise, and even extended walks and hikes present no problem for them. In the country they even enjoy pursuing mice and rabbits.

Breed-related problems: Because of the broad range of possible weights, there are

extremely tiny and very robust specimens.

The papillon and the phalène have a tendency to suffer from kneecap dislocations.

Pekingese

1. With good care, a healthy Pekingese can often reach the age of 17. It is very choosy in its dealings with humans, and it bestows its love and affection on a select few.

1. A Pekingese can be extremely obstinate.

1. Pekingese

Only the imperial family in ancient China had the right to breed these little lion dogs. The first Peking palace dogs came to England in 1860.

Appearance: Everything about this dog is broad: its head, muzzle, chest, and body. Many of its features are extreme: its large eyes, long-fringed ears, short, wrinkled muzzle, profuse coat of hair, bowed legs, and rolling gait.

Size and weight: Height at the withers, 6 to 10 inches (15–25 cm); weight, 11 pounds (5 kg) for males and 12 pounds (5.5 kg) for females.

Coat and color: Coat of hair with thick undercoat and rather coarse, long top coat. Heavy feathering on ears, legs, and tail. All colors are allowable, even brindle specimens with regular distribution of colors.

Temperament: Very self-assured and strong-willed. This dog does not bestow its affection on everyone, by a long shot. Mistrustful when faced with something unfamiliar. Not a typical family dog.

Grooming: Brush and comb daily. Males keep their full coat of hair throughout the year, while females shed during estrus. Clean facial wrinkles and eyes daily.

Care: Possible even in a small apartment. Long walks are not necessary. It needs consistency in training. Not infrequently a Pekingese will live to an age of 17.

Breed-related problems: Difficulty in whelping. Heavy breathing in hot or humid weather, because of the extremely short nose. Sensitive eyes.

2. Poodle

Dogs resembling poodles were known even in antiquity. Since the sixteenth century, they have been included in many paintings. Around 1900

Poodle

2. Poodles are bundles of high spirits, always in the mood for a game. Unlike the poodle pictured at right, the dog above has a conservative "canine coiffure."

2. This professionally styled hairdo is called a "fashion clip."

the first poodle breeders' associations were established in Germany. After World War II the poodle became a fashionable breed in Europe.

Appearance: The outward appearance depends largely on the clip. In the classic clip only the hindquarters are shorn completely. The cut currently in vogue shows the dog's athletic build to advantage.

Size and weight: Scarcely any other breed can offer such diversity. Toy poodle: height at the withers, 11 inches (28 cm); miniature poodle, 11 to 14 inches (28–35 cm); small poodle, 14 to 18 inches (35-45 cm); large

poodle, 24 inches (60 cm). Weight: not specified.

Coat and color: The dense, woolly coat of hair is fine-textured and uniform in length. It forms curls that have an elastic feel. The poodle does not lose any of its hair. The colors range from black through brown, apricot, and silver to white. There are also particolored poodles, either black and white or black with red.

Temperament: Very high-spirited, intelligent, adaptable, and easy to train. It is an outstanding watchdog, but never becomes aggressive. Black poodles are even-tempered, but with the sil-

ver and apricot-colored poodles, their temper sometimes gets the better of them. The easiest to teach are the brown members of the breed.

Grooming: Comb and brush daily. The poodle has to be trimmed about every four weeks. Clean the drooping ears regularly.

Care: Toy and miniature poodles are content in any environment. They love extensive walks. Watch out: Sometimes their innate drive to hunt reappears.

Breed-related problems: Kneecap dislocations.

Schipperke, Scottish Terrier

1. The schipperke is a watchful guard.

2. Scottish terriers need consistent, firm training.

tapering to a point. Born without a tail or docked.

Size and weight: Height at the withers not specified. Weight: small schipperkes, about 6.6 to 9 pounds (3–4 kg); medium-sized, 9 to 11 pounds (4–5 kg); large, 11 to 20 pounds (5–9 kg).

Coat and color: Hard, short coat of hair with ruff at neck and nape. On hind legs, coat forms "culottes." Deep black in color.

Temperament: It has the aptitudes of a watchdog; it is agile, lively, and inquisitive. Patient and kind with its family and with children. With strangers, reserved to unfriendly.

Grooming: Clean the dirt-resistant coat with a damp cloth. Bathe only when necessary.

Care: The small and medium-sized specimens are very suitable as apartment dogs. The large ones need a great deal of exercise outdoors.

2. Scottish Terrier

In the late nineteenth century the first Scottish terriers were exhibited at English dog shows. Soon thereafter these dogs were also bred in the rest of Europe, where the Scottie quickly became the "in" dog.

Appearance: Elongated head with ears carried erect, bushy eyebrows, and short beard. Large, round feet.

Size and weight: Height at the withers, 10 inches (25.5 cm); weight, about 15 to 23 pounds (7–10.4 kg).

Coat and color: Double coat of hair, with a short, soft undercoat and a smooth, hard top coat. Colors: black,

1. Schipperke

This breed originated in Belgium. The little "scheperke" (Flemish: small sheepdog) was mentioned in writing as early as the Middle Ages. It can be seen in many Flemish paintings. On farms and barges, this dog prevented rats and mice from spreading. In addition, it served as a watchdog.

Appearance: Head resembles that of spitz. Small ears, carried erect; dark, oval eyes; muzzle

Shih Tzu

3. The Shih Tzu's "lion's mane" should be tied together on the top of its head.

wheat-colored; brindled in many color gradations.

Temperament: Attentive and bright, sensitive and full of spirit, vigilant and mistrustful of strangers. Very stubborn—firmness in training is essential. Then the dog will behave well and show great understanding for its owner.

Grooming: Brush and comb its coat daily. Trim regularly.

Care: The Scottie is satisfied in an apartment, if it has a chance to fulfill its need for exercise.

3. Shih Tzu

This breed originated in Tibet. Many legends are centered around the breeding of these temple dogs in Asia over the course of several millennia.

Appearance: Long, thick coat of hair; tail carried over the back. Large, round eyes that have a mysterious look.

Size and weight: Height at the withers, up to 10.6 inches (27 cm); weight, 10 to 18 pounds (4.5–8.1 kg).

Coat and color: The long hair, which is equipped with an undercoat, should touch the ground without noticeable curls. All colors are permissible.

Temperament: It is friendly and independent. When playing, it is lively and attentive.

Grooming: Daily brushing and combing of hair; bathe once a month. Clean eyes and ears daily. Clean beard hair after meals.

Care: Makes a good apartment dog. It is content to lie in its customary spot. Don't lend support to its inclination to be a "home-body," because it can be quite a tireless runner.

Breed-related problems: The short nose with its small nostrils causes difficulty in breathing during hot weather.

Silky Terrier

1. Silky Terrier

This dog's forebears were taken along to Australia by English immigrants, where the little terriers were meant to hunt mice and other small animals. On the continent of Australia, they gave rise to two breeds: the wire-haired Australian terrier and the silky terrier.

Appearance: The silky is distinguishable from the Yorkshire terrier by its larger ears, more prominent muzzle, and longer back. In addition, it carries its tail higher and has hair of a slightly different color and length.

Size and weight: Height at the withers, 9 inches (23 cm); weight, 7 to 10 pounds (3.5–4.5 kg).

Coat and color: The silky hair, which is parted from the head to the root of the tail, falls smoothly on both sides. Hair length: 5 to 6 inches (13–15 cm).

Color: blue or bluish gray, silvery white or light blond on the head.

Temperament: Keenly alert, intelligent, lively, and robust. Friendly and affectionate with its owner and family.

Grooming: Daily brushing. Bathe once a month.

Care: An ideal apartment dog, provided it gets proper exercise outdoors. It is easy to train.

2. Tibetan Spaniel

These little "lion dogs" lived in Tibetan monasteries. They turned the prayer wheels or sat guard on the monastery walls and reported anything out of the ordinary. The first Tibetan spaniels came to England at the end of the nineteenth century.

1. The silky terrier is often confused with the Yorkie.

Appearance: The Tibetan spaniel cannot deny its kinship with the Peking palace dog, or Pekingese. Its head, which is small in proportion to its body, is proudly carried. Expressive dark brown eyes, oval in shape. Short legs. The tail is set high on the body and carried over the back.

Size and weight: Height at the withers, 10 inches (25 cm); weight, 9 to 15 pounds (4–7 kg).

Coat and color: Thick coat with silky texture and undercoat. The ears, the backs of the legs, and the tail are abundantly feathered. A pronounced mane is formed around the neck. All colors are allowed, with shades of brown being the most common.

Temperament: Like all other Asiatic dogs, the Tibetan spaniel has an unusual, almost catlike personality. It is intelligent, good-natured, and affectionate. It is mistrustful and aloof with strangers, sometimes aggressive as well.

Grooming: Brush and comb coat of hair regularly.

Care: Good for keeping in small apartments, but it needs lots of exercise.

3. West Highland White Terrier

The "Westie" belongs to the group of Scottish terriers and was originally used for hunting predators. A Landseer painting dated 1839 is evidence that white terriers were in existence as early as the beginning of the nineteenth century. In the painting we see a bloodhound and a white terrier, looking out together from inside a dog house.

The Westie became quite well known as the partner of a Scottish terrier in the advertising campaign for "Black & White" whisky. The models were terriers belonging to the whisky baron Buchanan, who had the dogs sketched in 1892. In 1906 the Westie was officially recognized as a separate breed.

Appearance: Round head with small ears and dark eyes, short muzzle, in combination with a jaunty look in its eye and the expression of a hardy terrier. Compact body, powerful legs, and a tail carried with self-assurance.

Size and weight: Height at the withers, 11 inches (28 cm); weight, 15 to 20 pounds (7–9 kg).

Coat and color: Double coat of hair: a hard top coat about 2 inches (5 cm) long and a soft, thick undercoat. Color: pure white.

Temperament: The Westie is alert, courageous, and self-assured, but not a yapper; very eager for exercise; friendly, cheerful dog for children.

Grooming: Daily brushing. The coat has to be trimmed professionally every three months.

Care: It needs plenty of exercise outdoors, a great deal of affection, and firm, consistent training. Then it is also possible to keep a Westie in an apartment.

Breed-related problems: Overly soft woolly or curly coat of hair. Too many missing teeth in the second set of teeth. Because the Westie is currently very much in fashion, many of them are being bred. As a result, often too little attention is paid to selecting dogs with excellent traits for breeding. Many of the animals are aggressive. For this reason, be careful in your choice of breeder when you buy a dog.

2. Exercise is very important for the Tibetan spaniel.

3. The Westie has a special "connection" to children.

Italian Greyhound

1. The Italian greyhound looks delicate and fragile.

1. Italian Greyhound

Two thousand years ago, small greyhounds were already common in Greece. The breed reached Italy in the Middle Ages. The Italian greyhound was a favorite in the royal houses of Europe. Frederick the Great, King of Prussia, had as many as 40 greyhounds in his cages.

Appearance: Small, long-limbed dog. Everything about it looks delicate, like filigree work. Narrow, long head. Large, expressive eyes. The ears are carried thrown back and folded. The back is slightly curved. The tail, set low on the body, is carried low, between the hind legs.

Size and weight: Height at the withers, 12.6 to 15 inches (32–38 cm); weight, up to 11 pounds (5 kg).

Coat and color: The coat is very short and fine. All colors are allowed, except brindle markings and black-and-tan. White patches on the chest and feet are permissible.

Temperament: Strong personality. High-spirited, alert, and courageous. In unfamiliar surroundings and with strangers, very reserved and cautious. Greyhounds are not suitable for small children.

Grooming: The short coat requires little care. Almost no shedding.

Care: There is room in the tiniest apartment for this small, easily satisfied, healthy greyhound. With loving training, the greyhound is an obedient comrade that you can let off its leash to run when you take walks. Not infrequently, it can reach an age of 15 years.

2. Yorkshire Terrier

In the nineteenth century it was bred in Yorkshire, England, to keep houses free of rats and mice. Its appealing appearance, however, quickly made it a favorite of all levels of society.

Appearance: Hair that hangs down evenly and straight. The coat is parted from the bridge of the nose to the end of the tail. Erect posture, whereby it creates an impression of self-importance.

Size and weight: Height at the withers, 8 to 9.5 inches (20–24 cm); weight, 4 to 6 pounds (1.8–3.1 kg).

Coat and color: Long, silky coat of hair without an undercoat; gold-colored head and steel-blue mantle.

Temperament: Lively, intelligent, courageous, and well-balanced. Often one also encounters shy or nervous Yorkies. Either mistakes were made in these dogs' raising, or their owners used the wrong training methods or none at all, out of anxiety about their dog.

Grooming: Without consistent, time-consuming care the hair will not reach the desired

Yorkshire Terrier, Miniature Pinscher

3. *Despite its delicate build, the miniature pinscher is extremely robust. It was previously known as the rehpinscher, or "roe deer pinscher." The miniature pinscher is a vigilant dog, but its barking can unnerve people who are sensitive to noise.*

2. *The Yorkie is one of the most popular small dogs.*

length. Regular bathing is necessary.

Care: An ideal apartment dog. It also needs exercise, however, to stay healthy and vigorous.

Breed-related problems: Small litters. Woolly, dark coat of hair. Kneecap dislocation.

3. Miniature Pinscher

It belongs to the family of pinschers and schnauzers. Of German origin, the breed is about 300 years old. It was in great demand, particularly at the beginning of the twentieth century.

Appearance: Tapering, narrow head. Undocked ears, either V-shaped with "folding flap" or small and erect. Oval eyes that do not protrude. Docked tail.

Size and color: Height at the withers, 10 to 12 inches (25–30 cm); weight not specified.

Coat and color: Short, thick, closely adhering coat of hair. Of one color—brown—in a great variety of shades (ranging to stag red). Also black with red or brown markings.

Temperament: High-spirited, with a great desire to play. Affectionate and self-confident. It forms a close bond with its family. Mistrustful of strangers. An outstanding watchdog and companion, owing to its tenacity and receptiveness to teaching.

Grooming: Brush regularly. Bathe only when absolutely necessary. Remove loose undercoat hair with a damp cloth.

Care: Can be kept successfully even in relatively small apartments. Not at all demanding, but should get plenty of exercise outdoors.

Miniature Schnauzer

1. The miniature schnauzer approaches even large dogs without fear.

1. Miniature Schnauzer

At the end of the nineteenth century the miniature schnauzer was exhibited for the first time at a dog show in Frankfurt. It seems certain that the affenpinscher, which was far better known at the time, exerted some influence on its outward appearance. People wanted to breed a small-scale image of the schnauzer, with all its character traits.

Appearance: Powerful, stocky build. Compact rather than slender. The head is elongated. Oval, dark eyes with bushy eyebrows. Erect or folded ears, which are not docked. It has the typical rough whiskers on its jaws. Docked tail.

Size and weight: Height at the withers, 12 to 14 inches (30–35 cm); weight not specified.

Coat and color: Wiry, coarse, thick coat of hair. The colors are solid black, salt and pepper, blackish silver, and white. If the color is salt and pepper, white markings on the head, chest, and legs are undesirable.

Temperament: Spirited temperament in combination with reflective composure. Affectionate and loving with its family but mistrustful of strangers. Fearless, even when up against large dogs.

Grooming: Regular brushing and combing are sufficient, because it sheds few hairs. Bathing is necessary only in exceptional cases. Clean whiskers after meals. The dog has to be trimmed regularly.

Care: The miniature schnauzer is good for keeping in apartments. Relatively long walks are important. It also needs firm, consistent training.

2. Toy Spitz, Pomeranian
3. Small Spitz

In English-speaking countries the toy spitz is known as the Pomeranian, because the first little spitzes that reached England came from Pomerania. Because of Queen Victoria, they became favorites of ladies of the English nobility over one hundred years ago. About 1970, Pomeranians came to Germany and soon attained a secure position among the most popular dog breeds.

After initial difficulties, breeders succeeded in stabilizing the dog's size and placing it on a healthful basis. English and American breeders often use large bitches in order to obtain larger litter sizes. However, in Germany one continues to see both toy and small spitzes being born to imported Pomeranians.

Appearance: At first glance, you might think you see a small, round ball of hair on four legs approaching you. In reality, in the tiny body there still remains a fair amount of the cheeky German spitz that today continues to live up to its reputation as an inexhaustible and undemanding guardian of houses and apartments.

Size and weight: Height at the withers, 7 to 8.6 inches (18–22 cm); weight, 3 to 4.4 pounds (1.5–2 kg). The small spitz is 9 to 11 inches (23–28 cm) high at the withers and weighs correspondingly more.

Coat and color: The Pomeranian is double-coated, with a thick, cottony undercoat

Toy Spitz, Pomeranian, Small Spitz

and long, straight hair that sticks out.

There are self-colored specimens in white, black, brown, or orange. More rarely there occur specimens with gray shading or spitzes in which the color range extends from cream through black-and-tan to particolored. If the dog is particolored, however, the ground color has to be white.

Temperament: Attentive, lively, cheeky, jaunty, and very affectionate with their owners. Mistrustful of strangers. Quick to learn and easy to train. Even the tiniest spitzes make good guardians for houses and apartments.

Grooming: The spitz's hair is easy to take care of. If brushed the wrong way every day, it will always look neat.

Bathe no more than twice a year. Clean eyes and ears when necessary.

Care: Small spitzes can be kept in the tiniest apartment. They do not need much exercise outdoors. If you have a yard, taking daily walks is not necessary.

Breed-related problems: Small litter sizes (usually only two puppies per litter), dental problems (with increasing age, they often lose their teeth). Kneecap dislocation.

2. The toy spitz is known as the Pomeranian in English. Its coat of hair is easy to take care of, although it has a high-maintenance look.

3. The small spitz is slightly bigger than the toy spitz.

Index

Note: Numbers in **bold face** refer to photographs or drawings.

Useful Books

For further reading on this subject and related matter, consult the following books also published by Barron's Educational Series, Inc.

Health

Alderton, David: *The Dog Care Manual,* 1986.
Frye, Fredric: *First Aid for Your Dog,* 1987.
Klever, U.: *The Complete Book of Dog Care,* 1989.
Streitferdt, U.: *Healthy Dog, Happy Dog: A Complete Guide to Dog Diseases and Their Treatment,* 1994.

Education

Baer, T.: *Communicating with Your Dog,* 1989.
Baer, T.: *How to Teach Your Old Dog New Tricks,* 1991.
Ullman, H.J.: *The New Dog Handbook,* 1984.
Wrede, B.: *Civilizing Your Puppy,* 1992.

Useful Addresses

American Boarding Kennel Association
4574 Galley Road,
Suite 400A
Colorado Springs, CO 80915

American Kennel Club
51 Madison Avenue
New York, NY 10010
(212) 696-8200

American Society for the Prevention of Cruelty to Animals
424 East 92 Street
New York, NY 10128
(212) 876-7700

Canadian Kennel Club
2150 Bloor Street West
Toronto, Ontario
M6 540 Canada

United Kennel Club
100 East Kilgore Road
Kalamazoo, MI 49001
(616) 343-9020

Veterinary Pet Insurance
1-800-USA-PETS
In California:
1-800-VIP-PETS

The Author

Armin Kriechbaumer, who has bred small dogs successfully for a great many years, is the publisher of "Kleinhundewelt," a specialized periodical. He serves as a specialty judge at dog shows and is the author of Barron's pet owner's manual on Yorkshire terriers.

Acknowledgments

The author and the publisher are grateful to Mr. Reinhard Hahn for his professional advice on all legal matters concerning the keeping of dogs, and to Dr. Gabriele Wiesr for her perusal of the chapter "Preventive Health Care and Diseases." The author thanks Mr. Peter Machetanz, a specialist in small dog breeds, for his assistance in compiling the portrait section of this pet owner's manual.

The cover photos:

Front cover: Bichon frisé with typical dense and abundant coat, and happy expression.
Inside back cover: Three cotón de Tulears with children.
Back cover: This pug puppy wants to be near its mother.

Important Notes

This Barron's pet owner's manual deals with the purchasing and care of small dogs. The author and the publisher believe it is important to point out that the guidelines for dog owners presented here apply primarily to normally developed puppies from good breeders—that is, to healthy dogs with good character traits.

Anyone who adopts a full-grown dog needs to be aware that the animal has already been profoundly influenced by other human beings. New owners should observe the dog carefully, including its behavior toward humans in their scrutiny, and should meet the previous owner. If the dog comes from an animal shelter, it may be possible to get information on its background and characteristics there. Some dogs, as a result of bad experiences with humans, have behavior problems and possibly even a tendency to bite. Such animals should be taken in only by experienced dog owners. Even well-trained and closely supervised dogs sometimes may damage someone else's property or even cause accidents. It is in the owner's interest to have adequate insurance protection, and we strongly urge all dog owners to purchase a liability policy that covers their pet.

In addition, make sure your dog gets all the necessary immunizations and is wormed periodically (see page 52); otherwise, the health of humans and animals alike is placed at risk. Several diseases and parasites are communicable to humans (see page 54). If your dog shows any symptoms of illness, it is essential to consult a veterinarian. If you have questions about your own health, see your doctor and tell him or her that you keep a dog.

The Photographers:

Angermayer: pages 20 left, right, 21, 91 below; Animal Photography/Thompson: pages 4, 9, 64 left, right, 69 right, 73 above, below, 78 right, 80 right, 81, 82 left, 83 right, 85, 87 below, 89 left; Animal Photography/Willbie: pages 28, 72, 75, 77, 79, 87 above, 89 right, 90, 91 above; Cogis/Amblin: page 96/inside back cover; Cogis/Bougrain-Dubourg: pages 12/13 above; Cogis/Labat: inside front cover, pages 5, 13 below, 69 left, back cover; Cogis/Lanceau: pages 16, 36 above, below, 37, 45, 57, 66 above, 68 right; Cogis/Nicaise: pages 13 center, 32, 33; Cogis/Varin: pages 29, 48; Gorski: page 88; Hinz: page 60; Info Hund/Kramer: page 74 right; *Inter-topics:* pages 61, 76 above, 78 left; Jacana/D'Hotel Christiane: page 25; Jacana/Trouilett: page 84 below; Junior/Bárdics: page 82 right; Junior/Cogis: page 67; Reinhard: pages 76 below, 86; Silvestris/Sunset/Lacz: pages 24, 49, 70 right, 84 above; Silvestris/Wagner: page 83 left; WAPI/Nicaise: pages 12/13 below, 13 above, 53, 65, 66 below, 68 left, 70 left, 71, 74 left, 80 left; Wegler: front cover, pages 40, 41 left, right; Wothe: page 12, below left.

First English language edition published in 1994 by Barron's Educational Series, Inc.
English translation © Copyright 1994 by Barron's Educational Series, Inc.

Address all inquiries to:
Barron's Educational Series, Inc.
250 Wireless Boulevard
Hauppauge, New York 11788

Library of Congress Catalog Card No. 94-71601
International Standard Book No. 0-8120-1951-2

Printed in Hong Kong
567   9927   9